STRATEGY ON THE UNITED STATES SUPREME COURT

To what extent do the justices on the Supreme Court behave strategically? In *Strategy on the United States Supreme Court*, Saul Brenner and Joseph M. Whitmeyer investigate the answers to this question and reveal that justices are substantially less strategic than many Supreme Court scholars believe. By examining the research to date on each of the justice's important activities, Brenner and Whitmeyer's work shows that the justices often do not cast their certiorari votes in accord with the outcome-prediction strategy, that the other members of the conference coalition bargain successfully with the majority opinion writer in less than 6 percent of the situations, and that most of the fluidity in voting on the Court is nonstrategic. This work is essential to understanding how strategic behavior – or its absence – influences the decisions of the Supreme Court and, as a result, American politics and society.

Saul Brenner is a professor of political science at University of North Carolina, Charlotte. He has published extensively regarding fluidity in voting on the Supreme Court, strategic voting at the cert vote, and majority opinion assignment. In 2007, he was awarded the Lifetime Achievement Award by the Law and Courts Section of the American Political Science Association.

Joseph M. Whitmeyer is a professor of sociology at University of North Carolina, Charlotte. He has published concerning small-group processes in journals such as *Social Psychology Quarterly* and *Sociological Theory*. He has been a visiting professor at the University of Hokkaido (Japan) and at the University of Groningen (The Netherlands).

Strategy on the United States Supreme Court

SAUL BRENNER

University of North Carolina, Charlotte

JOSEPH M. WHITMEYER

University of North Carolina, Charlotte

CAMBRIDGE
UNIVERSITY PRESS

CAMBRIDGE UNIVERSITY PRESS
Cambridge, New York, Melbourne, Madrid, Cape Town, Singapore, São Paulo,
Delhi

Cambridge University Press
32 Avenue of the Americas, New York, NY 10013-2473, USA

www.cambridge.org
Information on this title: www.cambridge.org/9780521736343

First published 2009

Printed in the United States of America

A catalog record for this publication is available from the British Library

Library of Congress Cataloging in Publication data
Brenner, Saul, 1932–
Strategy on the United States Supreme Court / Saul Brenner, Joseph M. Whitmeyer.
p. cm.
Includes bibliographical references and index.
ISBN 978-0-521-51672-3 (hardback) – ISBN 978-0-521-73634-3 (pbk.)
1. United States. Supreme Court – Decision making. 2. Judicial process –
United States. I. Whitmeyer, Joseph, 1960– II. Title.
KF8742.B727 2009
347.73'26–dc22 2008041377

ISBN 978-0-521-51672-3 hardback
ISBN 978-0-521-73634-3 paperback

Saul Brenner dedicates this book to his beautiful and talented grandchildren, Noam, Jonah, and Adira.

Joseph M. Whitmeyer dedicates this book to Rosemary.

Contents

[vii]

Contents

Preface

Since 1958 (Schubert, 1958) and particularly since 1989 (Marks, 1989), a host of Supreme Court scholars have advanced various strategic models in an attempt to explain why the Supreme Court justices behave the way they do. The purpose of this book is to introduce a great deal of the Supreme Court strategic research to undergraduate and graduate students, to evaluate it, and, at times, to present an original perspective regarding the topics covered by it. Strategic scholars, for example, typically view the majority opinion as a product of bargaining among the justices. In Chapter 8 of this book, however, we use the data supplied by Maltzman, Spriggs, and Wahlbeck for the Burger Court (2000) and show that there was very little individual bargaining over the content of the majority opinion on that Court. In addition, the conventional wisdom is that the individual justices pursue an outcome-prediction strategy; in other words, they vote to grant cert when they expect to win at the final vote on the merits and vote to deny cert when they expect to lose. In Chapter 5, we examine the prior literature, present some new findings, and conclude that there is much less support for this model than many strategic scholars believe.

We have attempted to write a book that can be understood by students who may lack a good methodological background but who are willing to make the effort of following a theoretical argument.

Although we have learned a great deal from many of the sources listed in the reference section, this book is particularly dependent on the prior research and theoretical discussion of eight scholars: Larry Baum, Lee Epstein, Jack Knight, Forrest Maltzman, Jeffrey Segal, Harold Spaeth, James Spriggs, and Paul Wahlbeck. These scholars have been the main protagonists in the debate regarding the value of strategic models for the study of Supreme Court decision making. We believe that the field of judicial behavior would have been substantially less sophisticated and informative if these scholars had chosen, instead, to become Wall Street lawyers or stand-up comics.

The two authors of this book come from very different backgrounds. Saul Brenner received a law degree from

Columbia Law School and a Ph.D. in political science from New York University. He has been publishing articles concerning Supreme Court decision making since 1975 (Brenner, 1975).

Joseph M. Whitmeyer has a Ph.D. in sociology from the University of Washington. Most of his research has concerned behavior in small groups in general. He began publishing articles regarding Supreme Court decision making only recently.

The authors of this book have submitted a longer version of Chapter 10 to a political science journal for possible publication.

We want to thank the following scholars for their critiques of earlier versions of this book: Ted Arrington, Larry Baum, Ken Godwin, Timothy Hagle, Eric Heberlig, and John Szmer, as well as the anonymous reviewers.

Finally, we thank Ed Parsons of Cambridge University Press for his help and encouragement, Susan Sweeney for her excellent editing, and Barbara Walthall of Aptara, Inc., for guiding this project through production.

Part I

Introduction

CHAPTER ONE

The Legal Model

Why do the justices on the United States Supreme Court behave they way they do? In an attempt to answer this question, Supreme Court scholars have posited three theoretical models: the legal model, the attitudinal model, and various strategic models.

Models, according to Segal, Spaeth, and Benesh (2005, p. 20), are "a simplified representation of reality. They do not constitute reality itself. A good model serves two contradictory purposes: It accurately explains the behavior in question and it does so parsimoniously, that is, sparingly or frugally." One can always maintain that a given model explains the behavior, but in science we expect models to be testable or falsifiable. A simple model might be easier to test and may be accurate enough especially when used to explain behavior averaged over a large number of people or for a long period of time. The legal model is the traditional, nineteenth-century explanation of why the justices behave the way they do. Advocates of this model posit that the justices decide cases based on their interpretation of the relevant legal materials. These materials include the U.S. Constitution, federal and state statutes, local ordinances, and the Court's precedents.

The legal model is insufficiently explanatory of decision making on the Court because the justices usually have to interpret ambiguous legal texts and it is uncertain how they ought to do so. Let us assume, for example, that the Supreme Court has to decide whether the use of lethal injections as a means for imposing capital punishment constitutes "cruel and unusual punishment" in violation of the Eighth Amendment to the U.S. Constitution. Should the justices focus on the text of the constitutional language? If they do, should they use the meaning of that text at the time the Eighth Amendment was adopted or should they use today's meaning? Whichever time period they choose, what sources should they examine to determine the meaning of the text? Should they examine public opinion, the opinion of elites, or the opinion of those who drafted this provision of the Constitution? What sources should they use to obtain this information? It is even uncertain as to who are the drafters of a provision of the Constitution. Is it the person or persons who wrote the language, the framers who voted for it, or the men who voted for the Constitution in the various states? Should the justices care about the purpose of the provision or the purpose of the Bill of Rights as a whole? How much attention should the justices pay to how prior Courts have interpreted this provision? There are no good obvious answers to these questions. Because there are no good obvious answers, this model cannot be tested and, thus, cannot be shown to be true or false.

Because the law is ambiguous, Segal and Spaeth (2002) reject the legal model. In place of this model, they argue that the justices vote their attitudes. We contend, however, that even though the law usually is ambiguous in the cases decided by the Court, a legal argument in favor of one side is often stronger than a legal argument in favor of the other side and that the strength of the legal argument is likely to be one of the variables influencing the justices' decision in a given case.

What characteristics should we associate with a strong legal argument? First, like all strong arguments, a strong legal argument ought to be coherent, complete, and consistent with our understanding of the real world. Second, it should be consistent with the relevant precedents or present a good reason why these precedents should not be followed or extended. Third, a strong legal argument ought to be based on an intelligent understanding of the relevant legal text. Fourth, it should be based on a favorable factual situation. Finally, for most justices, a strong legal argument ought to support an outcome and rule of law that will enable the Court not only to present a principled resolution of the question involved in the case, but also to establish a workable standard for future cases.

Until now we have advanced arguments both in favor of the legal model and against it. Can we posit a legal model that also recognizes the fact that the justices are influenced by their attitudes? Braman and Nelson (2007) have done so. They maintain (2007, p. 942) that the justices "really do use the law in thinking through cases, though their preferences [or attitudes] may influence the kinds of arguments and evidence they find persuasive." Braman and Nelson further maintain that there are limits to the extent to which the justices' decisions are based on "motivated reasoning" (i.e., reasoning influenced by their attitudes). Indeed, the "legal training and socialization of judges . . . includes constant reinforcement of the norm that it is *wholly inappropriate* for unelected jurists to impose their own beliefs on their decisions" (p. 941). Thus, we might expect that in some cases a given justice will interpret the relevant legal materials without regard to his attitudes. He would, instead, vote for the litigant with the stronger legal argument. Braman and Nelson's argument was influenced by their understanding of cognitive psychology.

It is too easy to adopt this alternative understanding of the decision making by the Supreme Court and conclude that the justices follow the legal model. Our job, if we want to be persuasive, is to indicate whether legal variables are influential even if we accept the view of Segal and Spaeth that the legal model has to be compared with an attitudinal model. More specifically, they argue that when a conservative justice votes for the conservative outcome in a given case and offers a legal justification for the outcome he favors, we should assume that he is voting his attitudes and not assume that his vote was a product of legal interpretation.

Some Supreme Court scholars have attempted to address this issue and have concluded that precedent influences the justices' votes. Richards and Kritzer (2002) and Kritzer and Richards (2003, 2005), for example, examined decision making at the final vote on the merits in three narrow areas of the law – freedom of speech, the establishment (of religion) clause, and search and seizure cases. They discovered that the attitudes of the justices and various case characteristics (usually called "case stimuli") significantly affected the voting of the justices, but they also found that the justices voted differently whether they were voting prior to or after a key landmark decision. In addition, in a major book-length study of the 1946 to 1999 era of the Court, Hansford and Spriggs (2006) discovered that the Court's interpretation of precedent was based not only on the attitudes of the justices but also on the extent to which the precedent was treated favorably in past decisions. Based on these four studies, it is reasonable to conclude that precedent influences the justices' decision making, even if we do not adopt the legal model advanced by Braman and Nelson.

It is uncertain, however, whether aspects of the legal model other than precedent are influential. Baum (2007, p. 120) maintains that "the law in general ... channels the justices' choices, often in subtle ways." In support of this statement, one might point to those cases in which a justice interprets a federal statute in a certain way while urging Congress to change the statute (see Hausegger and Baum 1999). In these cases it is reasonable to assume that the justices did not favor the decision they handed down but believed that they were compelled to so rule. This kind of activity, however, does not occur often on the Court. Also, in a recent study Howard and Segal (2002) sought to ascertain whether the justices on the Court are influenced by the original meaning of the constitutional text or by the intent of the framers of that text. They examined eight terms of the Supreme Court and discovered that the liberal and conservative justices were likely to support the arguments made by the attorneys from their preferred sides. In other words, they did not find any evidence that this aspect of the legal model was influential.

Because the legal model in its entirety has not been shown to be influential in determining the justices' final votes, and because other variables (such as attitudes) are likely to be influential, this model is simply not sufficiently useful for explaining decision making on the Court. Scholars, therefore, have turned to other models for this purpose.

Before you read about the first of these other models, it is necessary to know about the various stages in Supreme Court decision making. To facilitate this goal, we urge you to read Appendix 1 of this book.

CHAPTER TWO

The Attitudinal Model

In reaction to the weaknesses of the legal model, Pritchett (1948) proposed an attitudinal model. This model was the dominant model for explaining the final vote on the merits from the 1950s until the end of the 1990s. Some scholars (Segal and Spaeth, 2002) believe that it is still the dominant model for explaining this vote. It is widely accepted among Supreme Court scholars (or at least among most political scientists) that the attitudes of the justices are the most important determinants of why some justices confronted with the same set of cases vote for the liberal outcome, whereas other justices vote for the conservative outcome. Baum (2007, p. 149), for example, concluded that

Of all the considerations that could influence the Supreme Court decisions [at the final vote on the merits], I have given primary emphasis to the justices' policy preferences. The application of the law to the Court's cases is usually ambiguous, and constraints from the Court's environment are generally weak. As a result, the justices have considerable freedom to take positions that accord with their own conceptions of good policy.

Segal and Spaeth (2002) present an even more elaborate explanation of why the justices can be expected to cast sincere, attitudinal votes at the final vote on the merits. They tell us that (1) the justices possess lifetime tenure; (2) they hold highly prestigious jobs and, therefore, rarely seek higher office; (3) the justices constitute an independent, strong branch of the federal government and usually do not have to worry about the possible reaction of Congress or the president to their decisions; (4) there is a "reservoir of public support" for the Court (Segal, Spaeth, and Benesh, 2005, p. 35); (5) the Court is a court of last resort (unlike the highest state court and the U.S. Court of Appeals, decisions of the U.S. Supreme Court cannot be appealed to a higher court); and (6) the justices have virtually complete discretion regarding which cases they wish to decide, and they use this discretion to decide cases that offer plausible legal arguments on both sides and, therefore, give them the freedom to vote their attitudes. Posner (2008, p. 371) argues that legalist voting is especially less likely to take place in constitutional cases, for "the Constitution is vaguer than most statutes and in some respects embarrassingly obsolete."

The arguments of Baum, Segal, Spaeth, and Posner, however, do not suggest that the "liberal" justices on the Court will always vote for the liberal outcome and that the "conservative" justices will always vote for the conservative outcome. The facts in the case count, as the attitudinal scholars recognize. Based on the facts in the case, it is much easier for the justices to vote for the pro–free speech outcome in some cases than in other cases.

Other variables count as well. Collins (2008) examined the justices' voting at the final vote on the merits in the 1946 through 1996 era of the Court and discovered that a justice was more likely to cast consistent ideological votes (1) when the justice held overall extreme scores (an unsurprising finding); (2) the longer her tenure on the Court; (3) in salient cases; (4) when there was less interest group involvement in the case; and (5) the longer the tenure of the natural court.[1] Justice Scalia, for example, cast conservative votes in 62 percent of the non-salient cases, but in 78 percent of the highly salient cases. Justice Rehnquist, while a member of the sixth

---

[1] A "natural" court is a court in which the same justices are members throughout the period.

natural Burger Court (1975–1980), cast 70 percent conservative votes in the first 100 cases decided by the Court and 78 percent conservative votes in the remaining 756 votes.

Segal and Spaeth are mainly interested in explaining why the justices vote the way they do at the final vote on the merits. Attitudes, however, also influence other decisions of the Court – whether to grant or to deny a petition for a writ of certiorari, which outcome to favor at the conference vote on the merits, who is assigned to write the majority opinion, and whether to join that opinion or to write or join a concurring or a dissenting opinion. As Benesh (2003, p. 121) stated, " ... no one now studying the Court could presume to understand its decisions without reference to its attitudinal makeup ... "

An important aspect of the attitudinal model is the way that scholars conceptualize it spatially. Scholars envision a single dimension from extreme liberal to extreme conservative, represented as a line, and assume that each justice's attitude can be placed somewhere on the line. A justice's position on the line is usually called the justice's "ideal point." The justices' attitudes may vary according to the specific issue involved in a case. A justice may be somewhat liberal in search and seizure cases, for example, and somewhat conservative in cases concerning federalism. For this reason, scholars usually divide the cases into different issue areas and determine each

Figure 2.1. Percent liberal voting in civil rights cases of justices on first Rehnquist Court (9/86–2/88). M = Marshall, Br = Brennan, Bl = Blackmun, St = Stevens, P = Powell, O = O'Connor, W = White, Sc = Scalia, R = Rehnquist.

justice's ideal point in each issue area. To illustrate, Figure 2.1 shows the percentage of cases on which the justices on the first natural Rehnquist Court (September 1986–February 1988) voted for the liberal outcome in civil rights cases. These positions constitute estimates of the justices' ideal points in this issue area.

Limitations of the Attitudinal Model

Nevertheless, this model is limited in a number of respects. First, it is exclusively a Supreme Court model. Judges on the U.S. Court of Appeals, for example, often do not cast sincere, attitudinal votes because they feel compelled to vote in accord with Supreme Court precedent, if there is a relevant precedent in the case. Second, the attitudinal model is much less useful for studying the early Supreme Court, when a great majority of the Court's decisions at the final vote were unanimous.

[15]

It became particularly useful starting with the Stone Court (1941–1946), when the justices began to cast a large number of dissenting votes. Third, this model is pertinent only to orally argued and fully briefed cases. There are numerous summary decisions of the Court that are decided on the basis of a specific precedent. Fourth, the attitudinal model does not explain why some justices hold liberal views when appointed to the Court, whereas other justices hold conservative views. Nor does this model explain why some justices change their overall attitudes during their tenure on the Court. Fifth, this model mainly pertains to the final vote on the merits and not to the content of the majority opinion. Yet even Segal and Spaeth (2002, p. 357) recognize that the latter is usually more important:

> The decision on the merits merely indicates whether the . . . [lower court ruling] is affirmed or reversed and, consequently, which party has won and which has lost. The opinion of the Court, by comparison, constitutes the core of the Court's policy-making process. It specifies the constitutional and legal principles on which the majority rests its decision; it guides the lower courts in deciding future cases; and it establishes precedents for the Court's own subsequent rulings . . .

Finally, the attitudinal model is insufficiently explanatory because variables other than attitudes and the facts in the case determine why the justices vote the way they do at the final vote. Among such variables are the variables identified by Collins (2008), legal variables (see Chapter 1), small group variables (Brenner and Dorff, 1992), greater willingness by the justices to vote for the outcome favored by the solicitor general (Segal, Spaeth, and Benesh, 2005, pp. 323–324), greater willingness by them to vote for the outcome favored by the attorney presenting the stronger oral argument (Johnson, Wahlbeck, and Spriggs, 2006), and strategic variables. Concerning the latter, Epstein and Knight (1998, p. 10) argue that

> Justices may be primarily seekers of legal policy, but they are not unconstrained actors who make decisions based only on their own ideological attitudes. Rather, justices are strategic actors who realize that their ability to achieve their goals depends upon a consideration of the preferences of other actors, the choices they expect others to make, and the institutional context in which they act.

Our critique of the attitudinal model is incomplete,[2] but we believe that is sufficient for us to conclude that the Supreme

---

[2] For other critiques of the attitudinal model, see Benesh (2003); Murphy, Pritchett, Epstein, and Knight (2006, pp. 641–644); and Gerhart (2008, pp. 71–77).

Court scholars who support it have hardly advanced an ideal model.

In the next chapter we will explore various attempts to suggest a better model, all of which are based on the assumption that the justices are strategic actors.

CHAPTER THREE

The Strategic Models

If the justices are "strategic actors," as Epstein and Knight (1998, p. 10) maintain, what is their goal? According to Baum (2006, p. 6) a strategic justice will want the Court and the government as a whole to adopt a legal or public policy that is as close as possible to the policy she favors. A strategic justice, for example, might vote to grant certiorari (i.e., vote in favor of the Court hearing and deciding the case), in part, because she expects the Court to adopt her preferred policy when it hands down its decision (see Chapter 5). In addition, a strategic justice might vote insincerely and with the majority at the conference vote on the merits because she believes that such voting might enable her to influence the content of the majority opinion and, thereby, obtain some damage control (see Chapter 6). Finally, a strategic majority opinion writer might be willing to modify her ideal opinion to attract four additional votes for it, so that she can hand down an authoritative Opinion of the Court (also called a majority opinion), instead of a plurality opinion (see Chapter 9).

In contrast, a sincere justice will vote in accord with his preferred legal or policy position without considering the influence of his vote on the legal or policy position that will be adopted by the Court or the government as a whole.

Supreme Court scholars disagree regarding the extent to which the justices on the Court are strategic actors. Epstein and Knight (1998) and Maltzman, Spriggs, and Wahlbeck (2000) so characterize the justices, whereas attitudinal scholars such as Segal and Spaeth (2002) emphasize the importance of sincere, attitudinal voting and downplay the amount of strategic behavior in the justices' decision making. Baum (1997), who takes a middle position, reminds us that the justices may "gain intrinsic pleasure of doing what they think is right in itself" (p. 98) and that voting sincerely may please the outside audiences that "share their views" (p. 99). Baum also tells us that "compromises needed to secure victories and avoid defeats can be galling to the justices" (p. 96). He also informs us (2006, p. 16) that it takes time and effort to behave strategically and that the justices are not always willing to allocate their scarce resources for this purpose. A justice, of course, has only one vote and often he cannot convince a majority on the Court to support his policy or legal position. The best a losing justice in a given case can do is to write or join a dissenting opinion and hope that his views will be persuasive in a future case. Some dissenting justices, however, have no hope that they will eventually win on the merits in some future case. This is true, for example, regarding the four justices (known as "the Four Horsemen of the Apocalypse") who continued to vote against a number of major New Deal statutes in the post-1937 era. All these justices could do was to express their outdated views.

Even if Supreme Court scholars disagree regarding the extent to which the justices behave strategically, there is widespread agreement that the justices are policy-oriented. Most scholars who posit strategic models assume that the justices are exclusively so. In the language of George and Epstein (1992, p. 325) the justices are "single-minded seekers of legal policy." The term "legal policy" is meant to include the variables associated with both the attitudinal and the legal models.

Social scientists who study strategic behavior usually will use a rational choice model of individual decision makers. Green and Shapiro (1994, pp. 12–17) tell us that rational choice theorists commonly agree on the following items.

1. "Rational action involves *utility maximization*. In other words, "when confronted with an array of options . . . [the actor or agent] picks the one she believes best serves her objectives."

2. "Certain *consistency* requirements must be part of the definition of rationality." First, it must be possible for an agent's available options to be rank-ordered." Second, the "preference orderings are transitive." That is to say, if "A is preferred to B, and B is preferred to C, then . . . A [is] to be preferred to C."

3. "Each individual maximizes the *expected* value of his own payoff, measured on some utility scale." "The focus on expected rather than actual utility is required by the fact that decision making often takes place under conditions of uncertainty."

4. "The relevant maximizing agents are *individuals*."

5. The rational choice models "apply equally to all persons under study – that decisions, rules, and tastes [and goals] are 'stable over time and similar among people.'"

The rational choice model has been criticized, however. A major criticism is that the rationality principle embedded in this model is not realistic. MacDonald (2003, p. 556), for example, tells us that

A significant body of evidence demonstrates that human beings rarely behave purposively, consistently, and with the goal of maximizing their expected utility. Many sociologists, for example, question the notion of purposive choice, arguing instead that a large portion of human behavior is the result not of purposive calculation but rather of social roles that define appropriate behavior.... Similarly, many social psychologists challenge the notion of consistent preferences and utility maximization, pointing out that human beings rarely possess consistent preferences... engage in 'satisficing' behavior rather than optimization... and routinely make cognitive errors in calculation.

MacDonald (2003, p. 556) asks, how damaging is this criticism? He gives two responses. First, he points out that some rational choice theorists contend that although "humans are not always rational, such action is infrequent and unsystematic." In other words, "human beings in most social situations behave in a manner that approaches rational action." We are not persuaded by this response.

Second, MacDonald notes that other rational choice theorists argue that, even if the assumptions underlying this model "are found to be at least partially incorrect," the hypotheses posited by these theorists may be accurate (2003, pp. 556–557). Whether this argument is credible depends upon how "incorrect" is the underlying model and the extent to which the hypotheses are wedded to this underlying model.

Whether this criticism is damaging or not, we believe that rational choice theorizing could be useful for conducting social science research because it forces the researcher to initially focus on whether the actor is behaving rationally (Campbell, 2001, p. 156). If, however, the researcher finds that the actor is not behaving rationally (which is likely to occur), the researcher can, then, look for other variables "that may help to increase the explanatory power of the model" (Schotter, 2006, p. 510). If, for example, the researcher is interested in explaining why people vote in presidential elections, she might, first, explore whether the benefits of voting exceed its costs. Typically, the costs of voting consist of the time and effort it takes to register, to become informed about the candidates, and to vote, whereas the benefit of voting consists of the possibility of influencing the outcome of the election (Downs, 1957). When this explanation does not work, the researcher might, then, focus on such variables as duty or obligation to vote or the satisfaction in participation. Without rational choice theorizing, we might not have even asked why people vote. In fact, political scientists used to ask why approximately one half of the American people fail to vote in presidential elections.

In addition, there are other distinct advantages in using rational choice models.

1. These models help us to explore the microfoundations of human behavior, an important approach for understanding this behavior;

2. Rational choice models are typically formal models, in which the researcher attempts to set forth "in clear and transparent terms" the assumptions of the model (Schotter, 2006, p. 499);

3. These models often focus on strategic behavior, a topic that has been somewhat neglected in studying Supreme Court decision making;

4. Rational choice models often pose interesting research questions (e.g., Why does a given litigant seek certiorari when it is costly to file a cert petition and the chance of the Court granting certiorari and the litigant winning on the merits is exceedingly low? We will investigate this question in Chapter 4); and

5. This approach enables us to use the rich language and concepts of economics.[3]

Some of the rational choice models that we will investigate in this book are based on the assumption that the actors or agents will make decisions at a specific equilibrium point. The researchers who posit an equilibrium model assume that

---

[3] For an alternative discussion of the advantages of using rational choice models, see Baum (1997, pp. 133–135).

if each actor pursues the alternative that maximizes her utility, the group will arrive at an outcome such that no actor can better her situation by unilaterally changing her behavior. As a consequence, a specific outcome can be expected. As we describe in Chapter 9, for example, Rohde assumed that a majority opinion writer will seek an opinion that mirrors her views but would be willing to alter her ideal opinion to obtain four votes for it. The four justices will also seek an opinion that reflects their views as much as possible and will join the majority opinion if it is sufficiently modified to achieve their goal. In short, the opinion will be written at the appropriate equilibrium point. Similarly a willing buyer and a willing seller of a product in a competitive free market, each with perfect information and pursuing his self-interest, will execute their transaction at the appropriate price. Although we prefer rational choice models that posit a specific equilibrium point, we do not reject other models simply because they do not.

Other Goals of the Justices

If we assume that the justices are "single-minded seekers of legal policy" (George and Epstein, 1992, p. 325), our strategic models may be unrealistic because the justices often pursue other goals as well. Baum (2006, pp. 12–14) mentions three such goals: "pleasant working relations with colleagues," the avoidance of work or what Posner (1995, pp. 124–125) calls "the pursuit of leisure," and "the approval of individuals and groups that are important to them." Posner (2008, p. 36) states that judges seek "money, income, leisure, power, prestige, reputation, self-respect, the intrinsic pleasure . . . of the work, and the other satisfactions that people seek in a job." We believe that the justices on the Supreme Court are also interested in both efficient and legitimate decision making. The Court is concerned with immediate goals as well as future goals. At times, the Court has to sacrifice one goal to achieve the other.

Any one of these numerous goals might explain why a given specific strategic model does not explain the behavior. The casting of an insincere majority vote at the conference vote on the merits to obtain damage control (see Chapter 6), for example, might be viewed by the other justices as manipulative and exploiting the sincerity of these other justices and might strain working relations with them. In addition, a majority opinion writer who refuses to alter the language of his opinion, even though the requested change is a reasonable one, might also harm his relations with his colleagues. Also, trading votes between two cases to affect the outcome reached by the Court in these two cases (see Chapter 11) will not occur on the Court (even though it might benefit the two justices involved) because it conflicts with the justices' goal of legitimate decision making. Moreover, a majority opinion assigner will not always seek to assign the opinion to advance her policy or legal goals because she also has to be concerned about the Court's handling of its workload.

At times, it will make sense to incorporate one or more of these other goals into our strategic models, but at other times to do so would result in models that are too complex. If we do not incorporate these other goals, we ought at least to be sensitive to them when we evaluate the findings we obtain when we test our strategic models.

Part II

Certiorari

CHAPTER FOUR

The Losing Litigant Model

This book mainly focuses on the use of strategies by the justices of the United States Supreme Court. In this chapter, however, we preface this endeavor with a consideration of why a losing litigant might seek review at the Supreme Court level.

Why would anyone take a case to the United States Supreme Court? If one weighs costs and benefits, except for the unpaid or *in forma pauperis* petitions, the financial costs of submitting a petition for a writ of certiorari are large, and the chances of getting one's case heard are slim. In the 2004 term of the Court, for example, only 69 of the 2,041 paid petitions (3 percent) were granted cert (Epstein, Segal, Spaeth, and Walker, 2007, Tables 2–6). The percentage of the unpaid petitions was even lower (0.2 percent). Even if cert is granted, there is a good chance that the petitioner will lose on the merits. Epstein and Knight (1998, p. 27), for example, tell us that in the period from 1953 through 1994, the Court affirmed the decision of the lower court 38.7 percent of the time. It is certain that the financial costs will increase dramatically if cert is granted.

Despite these percentages, we can suggest why it might be rational for a litigant who has lost in the lower court to file a petition for a writ of certiorari. There has been little research on this topic to date, so for the most part we will reason theoretically.

First, for some losing litigants, the expected benefits of appealing are large. One reason may be that the litigants stand a better-than-average chance of getting their case heard by the Court and a good chance of winning on the merits as well. The most notable litigant fitting this description is the United States Government, almost always represented by the Office of the Solicitor General. The solicitor general has had a great deal of success before the Court both in terms of having its cert petitions granted and in terms of winning its cases on the merits. It can also appeal at a lower cost. The federal government, after all, pays the salaries of the attorneys in the Solicitor General's Office.

This argument suggests that we ought to discuss the principal-agent problem. There is a difference between the costs of the ultimate principal, here the taxpayers, and those of the principal's agent, here, the attorneys in the Solicitor General's Office.[4] Because the agent bears little or none of the costs of the litigation, the agent is likely to be more prone to litigate than the principal. The solicitor general, however, has the resources to file only a finite number of cert petitions in a given term and still do a good job with these petitions. Thus, he has to choose which cases he wants the Court to decide. Indeed, his ability to choose gives him the opportunity to select cases that are likely to be granted cert and likely to win at the final vote. Note that many attorneys in the Solicitor General's Office are former Supreme Court law clerks, who are keenly aware of what kinds of petitions are likely to be granted cert.

In a high stakes civil or criminal case, also, the expected benefits of appealing are large. If, for example, a civil case involves a large sum of money, the possible benefits of winning may indicate that it makes sense to file a cert petition. Indeed, as suggested by the study below, a losing litigant facing a prison term of any duration may consider even a small possibility of avoiding incarceration or reducing the amount

---

[4] Alternatively, we may consider the president to be the direct principal employing the agent. If so, the litigation may be at the principal's behest. But the president himself is the agent of the taxpayers, and he and his Solicitor General's Office together – the agent – may be more prone to litigation than the taxpayers – the principal.

of time he will have to spend in prison to outweigh the costs of litigation.

Second, for some losing litigants, the cost of petitioning the Supreme Court is low. The greater financial resources a petitioner has, the lower the costs of appeal will be in relative terms, and so the more likely he will appeal. *In forma pauperis* (unpaid) petitioners, who are excused from paying the costs of the cert petition because they are poor, and petitioners whose cases are sponsored by an interest group also should be included in this category. Unpaid petitions, however, are rarely granted cert by the Court (see the statistics mentioned earlier). For a collective body, such as a school district comprising many taxpayers or an interest group, the cost of litigation is divided among many people and, therefore, is low for each person. In many such groups, moreover, those who make the decision to litigate may themselves bear few of the costs (the principal-agent problem again). It is common, for example, for a small minority of a large group to make the decisions for the group (known as Michel's "Iron Law of Oligarchy"). The members of the controlling minority will personally bear few of the costs of litigation and will gain in status and power if the Court grants cert and they win on the merits.

Third, some losing litigants may attain important goals simply by appealing to the Supreme Court, regardless of the success of the appeal. Appealing to the Supreme Court may bring publicity to a group or person that seeks it. Murphy, Pritchett, Epstein, and Knight (2006, pp. 267–268), for example, tell us that the litigant activities of the National Association for the Advancement of Colored People (NAACP) Legal Defense Fund established this interest group as "the foremost organizational litigant" regarding civil rights for blacks. Appealing a case also may bring symbolic benefits. An appeal to the highest court may be a way for a person or group that has been convicted of a crime to publicly maintain their innocence. Elected or appointed governmental officials may appeal a case to demonstrate a particular political view that they believe will appeal to their constituents. This situation is likely to be compounded by the principal-agent problem, because the governmental officials, when acting on behalf of the government, do not themselves bear the financial costs of the litigation.

Regarding this third reason, some losing litigants can benefit from filing a cert petition because by doing so they will be postponing the payment of damages, a fine, the date when they will have to go to prison, or even their execution. This benefit could be crucial in a relevant case. Of course, if the Court grants cert they will benefit even more.

Fourth, some interest groups may sponsor numerous appeals, perhaps even simultaneously, in the hope that one or some will be granted cert by the Court and they will win on the merits. Some interest groups devote all or virtually all their resources to success in the Supreme Court. Alternatively, an interest group may decide which case or cases to sponsor and, thus, which ones to appeal to the Supreme Court based on whether the case offers a better chance of being granted cert and whether the interest group is likely to win on the merits if cert is granted. One of the explanations of the success of the Legal Defense Fund of the NAACP, for example, is that their attorneys were good strategists.

Fifth, some losing litigants may have overestimated their chances of winning (including the chance that the Supreme Court will grant cert and the chance the Court will reverse the decision of the lower court). Ignorance and inexperience of the litigant or her attorney probably play a role here. Another instance of the principal-agent problem may contribute to this mistake as well. Namely, the attorneys of the losing litigant may personally profit from an unsuccessful appeal, or at least will not bear its costs, and so may exaggerate the chances of success to the litigant.

Finally, some losing litigants may enjoy gambling even when the odds are against them. Alternatively, some losing litigants may be stubborn, that is, may find admission of defeat to be sufficiently aversive that they may find it worth the costs of appeal to delay such admission as long as possible.

There have been at least two published studies that focused on the conditions under which losing litigants are likely to seek cert. First, Songer, Cameron, and Segal (1995) inspected a random sample of search and seizure cases on the U.S. Courts of Appeals from 1962 through 1990. They discovered that the probability of winning, including the probability that the Court will grant cert, the probability that the losing litigant will win on the merits, and the availability of resources to the losing litigant are associated with his decision to seek cert, but the severity of the crime was not. Their first two findings support the first two reasons in the losing litigant model. Their third does not challenge this model, except to suggest that the criminal defendants probably perceive a possible prison term of any duration as a high stake.

Second, Zorn (2002) examined a random sample of decisions in which the federal government lost in the U.S. Court of Appeals during the 1993–1994 period. He discovered that three variables influenced whether the solicitor general would seek certiorari: the costs of the decision, its reviewability, and the likelihood of winning at the final vote on the merits. Concerning the first variable, Zorn assumed that cases in which the U.S. Court of Appeals invalidated a federal statute, regulation, or order were more costly to the federal government than cases in which this did not occur and that civil cases were more costly than criminal cases. Zorn found that both of these specific variables were related to whether the solicitor general sought cert. Additional studies, of course, are needed to investigate the other reasons given in the model.

CHAPTER FIVE

The Outcome-Prediction Strategy

Almost all of the cases heard and decided by the current Supreme Court come to the Court after it has granted a petition for a writ of certiorari. The Court grants this writ at its discretion.

Supreme Court scholars have identified a host of variables associated with the granting of cert by the Court. Caldiera and Wright (1988), for example, inspected the cases granted and denied cert during the 1982 term of the Burger Court and discovered nine variables that were associated with granting cert. The three most important were (1) the United States Government as a petitioner; (2) the presence of four or more amicus briefs in support of cert, indicating that the case was salient or important; and (3) the presence of an *actual* conflict between two or more lower courts or between the court immediately below and a Supreme Court precedent.

In addition, Cameron, Segal, and Songer (2000) examined a random sample of search and seizure cases between 1972 and 1986 and discovered that the Burger Court was likely to vote to deny cert when a conservative lower court had voted in favor of the criminal defendant. The conservative justices on the Burger Court probably reasoned that if a conservative lower court had voted in favor of the criminal defendant, the facts in the case were likely to be so strong in his favor that it was unnecessary for the Supreme Court to review that decision. This reasoning is similar to the argument that if the anti-Communist President Nixon was willing to go to China, it must mean that it is time for a change in American foreign policy. Cameron, Segal, and Songer called this behavior "strategic auditing," and we agree with their characterization.

Supreme Court scholars are not only interested in why the Court as a whole votes to grant cert. They also want to know why individual justices do so. Some scholars have argued that a justice is more likely to vote to grant cert when he expects that his preferred outcome (e.g., a reversal of the decision of the lower court) will win at the final vote on the merits and is less likely to vote to grant cert when he expects that his preferred outcome will lose at this vote. This behavior is called the outcome-prediction strategy. A justice can pursue this strategy to attain public policy goals, legal goals, or both. One of the justices on the Burger Court stated that he was following this strategy (*Time*, 1972):

> If I suspected a good decision by the lower court would be affirmed, making its application nationwide, I'd probably vote to grant. [On the other hand] a decision may seem outrageously wrong to me but if I thought the Court would affirm it, then I'd vote to deny. I'd much prefer bad law to remain the law of the Eighth Circuit or of the State of Michigan than to have it become the law of the land.

Murphy, Pritchett, Epstein, and Knight (2006, p. 629) argue that "It would be amazing if, as intelligent men and women, . . . [the justices] were not forward-looking and did not consider the implications of their cert vote for decisions on the merits, asking themselves: If I vote to grant a particular petition, what are the odds of my position winning down the road?" Whether these scholars are right is an empirical question.

Brenner (1979a) was the first scholar to examine the docket books of one of the justices (Justice Harold Burton) to determine whether there was a statistical relationship between the justice's cert votes and whether he was on the winning or losing side at the final vote on the merits. Brenner inspected the cases granted cert by the Court in the

1946, 1947, 1949, 1950, 1954, and 1955 terms. He discovered that the affirm-minded justices (i.e., those justices who voted to affirm the decision of the lower court at the conference vote on the merits in the individual cases) in the aggregate were likely to have followed this strategy, whereas reverse-minded justices were not. Brenner (1979a) argued that the reverse-minded justices had "so much to gain and so little to lose . . . that it was not worth their time and effort to calculate their chances of winning" when they cast their cert votes. These justices, after all, were confronting lower court decisions they disliked. The Court, in addition, was much more likely to reverse than to affirm. Thus, it made sense for these justices to gamble on the possibility that the Court will reverse. The affirm-minded justices, Brenner contended, were in a different situation. They were confronting a decision of the lower court that they liked. They risked the possibility that this decision will be reversed at the more authoritative Supreme Court level, and the Court was much more likely to reverse than to affirm. It certainly made sense for them to take the time and effort necessary to calculate whether the position they favored was likely to win or lose at the final vote prior to casting their cert vote.

In support of this argument, Brenner and Krol (1989) inspected seven terms in the Vinson, Warren, and Burger Courts and discovered that the affirm-minded justices who won at the final vote had a cert grant rate of 67.5 percent, whereas affirm-minded justices who lost had a cert grant rate of 39.1 percent, but reverse-minded justices who won actually had a lower cert grant rate than the reverse-minded justices who lost (cf. 77.3 percent vs. 82.1 percent). Subsequent scholars (see Boucher and Segal, 1995; Segal and Spaeth, 2002; and Segal, Spaeth, and Benesh, 2005) accepted Brenner's general conclusion that affirm-minded justices in the aggregate follow the outcome-prediction strategy, whereas reverse-minded justices do not. These scholars also accepted Brenner's explanation for this result.

Even if affirm-minded justices *in the aggregate* are engaged in outcome prediction, a large number of *individual* affirm-minded justices are not so engaged. We examined the behavior of the individual affirm-minded justices in the Vinson, Warren, and Burger Courts. We focused on the individual justices in these three Courts who cast at least 50 affirm votes in a given Court and discovered that only about half (52 percent) of them voted in accord with this strategy: Three of the ten justices on the Vinson Court did so (Black, Burton, and Frankfurter), nine of the thirteen on the Warren Court (Black, Brennan, Clark, Douglas, Frankfurter, Harlan, Reed, Stewart, and Whitaker), and five of the ten justices on the Burger Court (Brennan, Burger, Marshall, Rehnquist, and White). These results, together with the contrasting results for

Table 5.1. *Cert Grant Rates for Affirm-Minded Individual Justices on the Vinson Court*

Justice	Win at Final	Lose at Final	N
Black	54.3%*	34.6%	144
Reed	63.8	52.2	206
Frankfurter	56.0*	41.9	187
Douglas	71.6	67.4	120
Murphy	(81.1)	(90.0)	47
Jackson	46.4	53.2	172
Rutledge	57.4	63.6	58
Burton	60.9**	37.8	219
Vinson	49.0	35.3	185
Clark	71.6	62.5	75
Minton	48.4	33.3	79
TOTAL	58.2***	47.6	1492

Significantly greater using Fisher's exact test: $*p < .05$; $**p < .01$; $***p < .001$.

reverse-minded justices on the Burger Court, are shown in Tables 5.1, 5.2, and 5.3. We are not the only scholars who investigated this topic. Segal, Spaeth, and Benesh (2005, p. 289) discovered a *moderate* association between voting to grant cert and winning at the final vote for only three of the thirteen individual affirm-minded justices on the Burger Court (gamma coefficients of .37, .34, and .24) and a *weak* or *nonexistent* association for the other ten affirm-minded justices.

Table 5.2. *Cert Grant Rates for Affirm-Minded Individual Justices in the Warren Court*

Justice	Win at Final	Lose at Final	N
Black	58.7%*	43.2%	270
Reed	69.0**	40.5	108
Frankfurter	55.6***	28.8	235
Douglas	56.1***	32.6	250
Jackson	(78.6)	(50.0)	16
Burton	62.3	60.0	172
Clark	63.1**	42.2	381
Minton	46.3	34.8	90
Warren	71.8	56.0	241
Harlan	62.3***	40.5	412
Brennan	82.1***	73.3	188
Whittaker	48.8*	31.9	133
Stewart	60.0***	32.5	238
White	69.0	53.8	139
Goldberg	(87.5)	(100)	29
Fortas	(70.4)	(62.5)	35
Marshall	(81.3)	(100)	17
TOTAL	63.6***	41.3	2954

Significantly greater using Fisher's exact test: $*p < .05$; $**p < .01$; $***p < .001$.

Finally, Brenner, Whitmeyer, and Spaeth (2006) inspected the cases in which certiorari was denied by the Burger Court and discovered no evidence to suggest that the justices were engaged in outcome prediction. In most of these cases, the

Table 5.3. *Cert Grant Rates for Individual Justices in the Burger Court*

Justice	Affirm-Minded			Reverse-Minded		
	Win at Final	Lose at Final	N	Win at Final	Lose at Final	N
Black	(45.5%)	(33.3%)	37	73.1%	75.0%	56
Douglas	–	–	0	69.0**	51.4	347
Harlan	(73.3)	(71.4)	37	75.4	100	60
Brennan	46.1***	29.4	616	68.2	88.2***	644
Stewart	57.9	59.2	297	68.3	78.4	527
White	84.5**	66.7	471	86.8	92.5	872
Marshall	47.2***	25.4	577	65.0	76.8*	626
Burger	46.6*	33.3	378	71.8	82.0	767
Blackmun	64.5	62.8	474	80.4	83.6	729
Powell	68.5	61.5	363	78.9	88.7	740
Rehnquist	54.3***	29.7	358	84.7	96.4***	759
Stevens	36.6	28.6	358	70.1	84.9*	421
O'Connor	68.8	52.9	129	83.2	94.7	257
TOTAL	58.2***	38.3	4095	76.1	80.5**	6805

Significantly greater using Fisher's exact test: $^*p < .05$; $^{**}p < .01$; $^{***}p < .001$.

Court voted to deny cert by a unanimous vote. One suspects that, in most of these unanimous deny cases, the justices on the Court believed that the lower court handed down the right decision and the case was inappropriate for review (or, in other words, it was not certworthy). In this circumstance, of course, all nine justices cast cert votes contrary to the outcome-prediction strategy, for they voted to deny cert when they could have won at the final vote on the merits if cert had been granted.

In short, the evidence in favor of the outcome-prediction strategy is weak. Why is this true?

The Assumptions Underlying This Model

To answer this question, it is useful to examine the five assumptions underlying this model: (1) When casting her cert vote, an individual justice will assume that her cert vote might determine whether the Court will grant or deny cert; (2) she will be able to predict fairly accurately what outcome she will favor at the final vote on the merits; (3) she will also be able to predict fairly accurately what outcome the Court will vote for at the final vote on the merits; (4) her desire to win on the merits or to avoid losing will dominate her decision whether to vote to grant or deny cert; and (5) it is legitimate for her to vote in accord with this strategy.

All five assumptions can be challenged. First, it is unlikely that an individual cert vote will determine whether cert is granted.[5] If her vote will not determine the outcome, it is problematic whether a justice will be willing to pay the decision-making costs involved in pursuing this strategy.

Second, when casting her cert vote, a justice might be uncertain whether she will eventually want to affirm or reverse the decision of the lower court. The cert vote takes place prior to (1) the submission of the litigants' briefs on the merits; (2) oral argument; (3) the conference vote on the merits; and (4) the drafting of the various opinions. We know, of course, that some justices change their votes between the conference vote on the merits and the final vote, but at the time she casts her cert vote a justice could be uncertain regarding which outcome she will eventually favor even when she does not later shift to the other side.

Third, if a justice may have difficulty predicting his own merits vote, imagine how much more difficult it might be for him to predict the merits vote of the Court. The Supreme Court, after all, mainly hears "hard" cases, that is, cases in which there are plausible legal arguments on both sides.

Fourth, at various times, there will be a conflict between the outcome-prediction strategy and other reasons for voting to grant or deny cert. In these situations, it is uncertain

---

[5] A justice will be certain that her vote is crucial when there are three votes to grant cert and five to deny and the justice is voting last. In other situations, a justice's vote could be crucial if she can correctly predict how a colleague is likely to vote.

whether the desire to win at the final vote or avoid losing will dominate a justice's cert vote. In a large percentage of cert petitions, the case is uncertworthy (defined as inappropriate to be heard by the Court, at least as the standards are defined in that term). Also, in a certain percentage of cases, it would be irresponsible for the Court not to grant cert (Perry, 1991). The outcome-prediction strategy, if it is relevant, would be relevant only in the intermediate situation.

In addition, at various times the Court will grant cert to two cases from two circuit courts that were decided in conflict with each other. If an individual justice votes to grant cert in both cases (which may be the appropriate thing to do), he is likely to win on the merits in one of the two cases and lose in the other case.

Fifth, at least one scholar (Provine, 1980, p. 172) believes that the pursuit of the outcome-prediction strategy is illegitimate, or, in her language, "inappropriate."

Thus, it is not surprising that the outcome-prediction model often does not predict the justices' cert behavior, for the five assumptions on which this model is based are often inconsistent with our understanding of decision making at the cert vote.

This, however, is not the only kind of possible strategic behavior that might be pursued by individual justices at the cert vote. A justice might threaten to write a dissenting opinion from a denial of certiorari to persuade other justices to vote to grant cert (Epstein and Knight, 1998, p. 63). In addition, she may vote to "join three," that is, indicate that she is willing to vote to grant cert if three other justices vote to grant. If the justice in question voted this way with the expectation that the other justices would reciprocate in future cases, such behavior ought to be perceived as strategic (see Epstein and Knight, 1998, pp. 122–125).

Part III

The Conference Vote
on the Merits

CHAPTER SIX

Strategic Voting at the Conference Vote

For most of the Court's history, the justices used a two-stage procedure at the conference vote on the merits. In the first stage, the justices discussed the case and did so in order of seniority, with the chief justice speaking first. In the second stage, they voted and did so in the order of juniority, with the chief justice voting last. This procedure was ideal from the perspective of the chief justice. In the first stage he was in a good strategic position to persuade his colleagues how to view the case. In the second stage, he was ideally situated to vote with the majority if he so wished and, thereby, to assign the majority opinion. Chief Justice Hughes, for example, took advantage of this two-stage procedure (Dickson, 2001, p. 12). During the later years on the Warren Court, this procedure changed (Murphy, Pritchett, Epstein, and Knight, 2006, p. 633). The two stages were merged into one, and the justices both discussed the case and cast their votes in order of seniority, with the chief justice discussing and voting first.

Chief Justice Warren Burger, who came to the Court in 1969, was stuck with the new procedure. Yet he wanted to assign the majority opinion more often and was burdened with voting first. To solve this problem, Chief Justice Burger, at times, "passed" at his initial conference vote and voted with majority after all the other justices had voted. Presumably, some of Burger's conference votes were insincere (i.e., contrary to his ideological or legal position) and were cast to retain the opinion assignment and, thereby, gave Burger some control over the content of the majority opinion (Johnson, Spriggs, and Wahlbeck, 2005). The best way of obtaining some control was for Burger to either self-assign the majority opinion or assign it to an ideological ally. The extent to which Burger was able to obtain a majority opinion that he liked by using this method is uncertain. What is certain is that Burger's extensive "passing" was not appreciated by his colleagues and hurt his reputation. In short, his behavior was probably perceived as illegitimate by the other justices.

What mainly interests us in this chapter is not Chief Justice Burger's behavior but, rather, whether the associate justices on the Burger Court cast insincere majority conference votes. An associate justice might cast such a vote because she also was seeking damage control (i.e., seeking to control the content of the majority opinion so as to make it less offensive to her views). She might achieve this goal as the majority opinion assigner (as the senior associate justice in the conference coalition), as the majority opinion writer, or as a member of the conference coalition. The later a given justice votes in conference, the more easily she can cast an insincere majority vote. A justice who votes last will always know which side will win at the conference vote, whereas a justice who votes first, second, third, or fourth will never know, although he may be able to predict based on other information he may have regarding the past voting behavior of the other justices on the Court.

A host of Supreme Court scholars contended that the justices will cast insincere majority conference votes. O'Brien (2005, p. 257), for example, argued that

> At conference, a justice may vote with others if they appear to constitute a majority, even though he or she disagrees with their treatment of a case. The justice may then bargain and try to minimize the damage, from his or her policy perspective, of the Court's decision.

Similarly, Hammond, Bonneau, and Sheehan (1999, p. 53) concluded that

> A justice whose ideal point is on the minority side will vote with the majority side . . . [at the conference vote] if, in so doing, he or she can influence opinion assignment . . . (or) opinion writing in such a way that the outcome on the final vote on the merits is closer to his or her own ideal point.

And Maltzman, Spriggs, and Wahlbeck (2000, pp. 1–4) tell us that Justice Brennan voted insincerely in *Pennsylvania v Muniz* 496 US 582 (1990), so that he could self-assign the majority opinion and, thereby, prevent Justice O'Connor from writing an opinion that was likely to undermine the constitutional protection offered to criminal defendants by the *Miranda* decision. Justice Brennan sent a memo to Justice Marshall that revealed this fact.

Arrington and Brenner (2004) sought to determine the conditions under which an associate justice on the Burger Court voted with the majority at the conference vote. Not surprisingly, they discovered that ideology and case stimuli influence whether the justices voted with the majority at this vote. They failed, however, to find any evidence that the order of voting is related to whether the justices voted with the majority. In other words, the justices who voted later in the process were no more likely to vote with the majority than the justices who voted earlier. These two scholars also discovered that the individual justices, serving in two or more natural courts, did not join the majority more often when they voted later in the sequence. In short, Arrington and Brenner did not find any evidence that the associate justices cast insincere majority conference votes.

Why is it that the associate justices do not often vote with the majority and against their preferences at the conference vote to obtain damage control? We suspect that the justices do not do so because it is difficult to obtain any substantial amount of damage control in this way. If the associate justice is not the majority opinion writer, he would have particular difficulty. For why should the majority opinion writer attempt to satisfy the demands of justices who disagree with the outcome supported by the majority at the conference vote and, therefore, are probably making extensive demands for changes in the majority opinion, when it is much easier to attempt to satisfy the demands, if any, of the justices who favor this outcome? Indeed, if the majority opinion writer attempts to please the justices who disagree, he risks offending the other justices in the conference coalition.

Only if a justice is assigned to write the majority opinion might he be able to obtain some damage control. It is uncertain, however, that he will be able to get a great deal of control even under this circumstance. An associate justice, of course, cannot count on being assigned to write the majority opinion unless he is the opinion assigner.

Westerland (2003, p. 18) offers another reason why insincere majority voting to obtain damage control does not often occur on the Court. He states that such a strategy "would be easily detected, and the reputation cost would . . . [decrease] the offending justices' chances of being able to influence majority opinions." In short, such behavior is likely to be perceived as insincere or even illegitimate.

CHAPTER SEVEN

Fluidity and Strategic Voting

It is common knowledge that, at times, an individual Supreme Court justice will vote to reverse the decision of the lower court at the conference vote on the merits and will vote to affirm that decision at the final vote or the converse. In the Vinson Court era (the 1946 term through the 1952 term) and during the 1957–1967 period of the Warren Court, the individual justices switched their votes in 10 percent of the pairs of votes (Brenner, 1989) and in the Burger Court the percentage was 7.5 percent (Maltzman and Wahlbeck 1996, p. 587). There is not a great deal of fluidity in voting because "judges do not treat a vote, though nominally tentative, as a hypothesis to be tested by the further research conducted at the opinion-writing stage. That research is mainly a search for supporting arguments and evidence" (Posner, 2008, p. 110).

The question that interests us in this chapter is the extent to which the fluidity in voting constitutes strategic voting. Maltzman and Wahlbeck (1996, p. 581) conclude that

> Justices are strategic actors. This is particularly evident when they change their votes between the original conference on the merits and the Court's announcement of the final decision.

Baum (1997, p. 106), however, presents a mixed picture:

> Fluidity can result from strategic voting. But strategic voting may be reflected in the original conference vote. Further, changes in position can occur for reasons other than strategy. Justices may reevaluate the merits of cases on their own.... Even when justices change positions in response to interactions with colleagues, the impact of these interactions might be to provide information that clarifies the relationship between the justices' preference and the alternatives in a case.

Finally, Gillman (1999, p. 70) tells us that "the mere fact that a justice may have changed her mind [regarding which outcome to support] during the opinion-writing stage ... is not evidence of a strategic bargain."

To answer the question regarding the extent to which fluidity in voting constitutes strategic voting, it is useful to focus on the conditions under which fluidity is likely to occur.

Maltzman and Wahlbeck (1996) examined fluidity in voting on the Burger Court and discovered that fluidity in voting was most likely to take place under the following conditions:

1.   When a justice was ideologically closer to the justice writing the opinion for the coalition on the other side than to the justice writing the opinion for the coalition he voted with at the conference vote (Hypothesis 1);
2.   When a justice was ideologically closer to the coalition on the other side than to the coalition he voted with at the conference vote (Hypothesis 2);
3.   When the conference coalition was not minimum winning (MW); in other words, it was not 5–4 or 4–3 (Hypothesis 3);
4.   In complex cases (Hypothesis 4);
5.   When a justice was a freshman (Hypothesis 5);
6.   When a justice voted with the minority at the conference vote (Hypothesis 9a); and
7.   When a justice voted with the minority at the conference vote and there were only a few members in the minority (Hypothesis 9b).

How can we explain these findings? First, Hypotheses 1 and 2 (the ideological hypotheses) can be explained easily if we assume that the justice involved erred at the conference vote in matching her attitudes to the alternatives in the case, but was successful in doing so at the final vote.

Second, Hypotheses 4 and 5 (i.e., the complexity hypothesis and the freshman hypothesis) can be explained if we assume that the justice involved was uncertain regarding how to vote at the conference vote. Indeed, Maltzman and Wahlbeck (1996) explain these two findings in this way.

Third, Maltzman and Wahlbeck (1996) discovered that justices who dissented at the conference vote were more likely to switch to the other side than justices in the majority at the conference vote (Hypothesis 9a) and that the justices in the minority at the conference vote were particularly likely to switch when there were only a few members in the minority (Hypothesis 9b). There are numerous reasons why a justice in the minority at the conference vote may want to conform to the majority. She may be impressed that a majority of the justices voted for that outcome, she may want to be on the winning side, she may believe in the value of consensus, she might want her colleagues to view her as a "good team player" (Baum, 2006, p. 58), or she may not wish to take the time and effort necessary to write a persuasive dissenting opinion. None of these reasons are usually considered strategic reasons.

Finally, because members of MW conference coalitions are under great pressure to remain in the winning coalition, members of conference coalitions that are larger than MW are more likely to shift their votes (Maltzman and Wahlbeck, 1996) (Hypothesis 3). In short, none of the variables that explain the fluidity in voting ought to be viewed as strategic.

We not only want to examine individual fluidity in voting to determine whether it constitutes strategic voting. We also want to investigate dispositional fluidity, in other words, the shifting by the Court from affirm to reverse or the converse. Brenner and Spaeth (1988) inspected three terms of the Warren Court and discovered that the Court was more likely to switch to the other side when the conference coalition was MW (5–4 or 4–3) than when it was not (20 percent v. 1 percent). They also found that when an MW Court shifted to the other side, the marginal justice in the conference coalition (i.e., the justice ideologically closest to the dissenters) was a member of the final winning coalition in 86 percent of the cases. The question arises: Under what conditions is the marginal justice in MW conference coalitions likely to switch to the other side? Brenner, Hagle, and Spaeth (1989) addressed this question for the Warren Court. They discovered that the marginal justice was most likely to shift sides when

1. she was ideologically closer to the dissenters at the conference vote than to any member of the majority coalition;

2. she was less competent, as defined by the Blaustein and Mersky (1978) reputation polls;
3. the case was less salient;
4. the case was more complex.

None of these reasons suggests strategic voting. Rather, they suggest that the marginal justice either was uncertain regarding how to vote at the conference vote (items 1, 2, and 4) or did not devote sufficient time to vote correctly at the conference vote (item 3).

In other words, we have found alternative, nonstrategic reasons why fluidity in voting takes place. These include (1) a mistaken conference vote and (2) conformity voting. We also examined the findings of three other fluidity studies (Brenner and Dorff, 1992; Dorff and Brenner, 1992; and Hagle and Spaeth, 1991). None of the findings from these three studies suggest that fluidity in voting is necessarily strategic.

This is not to suggest that the justices will never shift for strategic reasons. We can suggest the following strategic reasons for shifting:

1. A justice in dissent at the conference vote might switch to the other side because his views have been accommodated by the majority opinion writer. Wahlbeck, Spriggs, and Maltzman (1996), however, tell us that the majority opinion writers on the Burger Court

rarely took seriously the suggestions or threats made
by the dissenters at the conference vote:

> ... when members of the majority conference
> coalition sent letters making suggestions, present-
> ing threats, or expressing their desire 'to wait',
> the number of opinion drafts that were circulated
> increased. Although a strategic author is likely to
> be concerned with threats and suggestions from
> members of the majority, we did not anticipate
> and did not find support for such an effect due to
> letters from members of the conference minority.

In a subsequent paper, Spriggs, Maltzman, and
Wahlbeck (1996) state the "justices who do not vote
with the majority coalition at conference have a min-
imal role in shaping the majority opinion." Thus, the
image of dissenting justices at the conference vote
switching to the other side because their views have
been accommodated in the majority opinion is hardly
a credible image.

2. Howard (1968) argued that one or more of the justices "frequently" changed his or their vote(s) so that
the Court could form a united front against an outside threat. Howard is describing what took place in
Brown v Board of Education 347 US 483 (1954). We
cannot think of any other case in the post-1946 era

when the Court faced a threat to its power or authority, reacted to that threat by forming a united front against the threat, and did so at the final vote but not at the conference vote. All three conditions must be present. As a consequence, it is unlikely that Howard has identified a situation in which there was a great deal of fluidity in voting. In *United States v Nixon* 418 US 683 (1974), for example, the Court was faced with a threat to its authority by President Nixon and formed a united front against the threat, but the justices voted 8–0 at both the conference vote and the final vote. Similarly, a large number of cases in which the Warren and early Burger Courts in the post-*Brown* era voted in favor of the black litigants claiming discrimination were decided unanimously at both votes.

3. A justice in dissent might shift because she believes that the writing of a dissenting opinion will increase the salience of the majority opinion. But if a dissenting justice is concerned about this possible consequence, she could dissent without writing a dissenting opinion.

4. A dissenting justice might agree to shift to the other side and join the majority opinion with the tacit understanding that the majority opinion writer will switch and join her opinion in a future case. We do

not believe, however, that this motivation for shifting occurs often. Indeed, there is no evidence that the justices who join other justices' majority opinions receive more votes for their opinions from these other justices (see Arrington and Brenner, 2008).

In short, even though we can imagine strategic motivations for a justice to vote for a different outcome at the final vote than he did at the conference vote, this is hardly the stuff of everyday decision making.

Part IV

The Majority Opinion and Other Opinions

CHAPTER EIGHT

The Extent of Successful
Bargaining over the Content
of the Majority Opinion

To what extent does the majority opinion writer alter his initial majority opinion to obtain the votes of the other justices? Baum (1997, p. 106) tells us that "it is standard practice [for the justices] to modify the language of opinions in an effort to win colleagues' support," and Maltzman, Spriggs, and Wahlbeck (1999, p. 55) inform us that

> Murphy (1964), Spriggs, Maltzman, and Wahlbeck (... [1999]), Epstein and Knight (1998) and others argue that justices *regularly* make suggestions and threats and even circulate separate opinions as a mechanism for extracting concessions from the majority opinion author. And, they show that majority opinion authors frequently respond to these bargaining strategies by altering the opinion. (Emphasis supplied by us)

We evaluate these statements in this chapter by examining the data supplied by Maltzman, Spriggs, and Wahlbeck (2000).

Maltzman, Spriggs, and Wahlbeck (2000) investigated opinion coalition formation on the Burger Court and discovered that the justices who dissented at the conference vote on the merits rarely sought any changes in the majority opinion, but when they did, their suggestions were almost always ignored by the majority opinion writer. Thus, if these justices shifted to the majority and joined the majority opinion, they almost always did so without getting the majority opinion writer to change his initial opinion. If any bargaining took place on this Court, it is much more likely to have taken place between the majority opinion writer and the members of the conference coalition. Maltzman, Spriggs, and Wahlbeck (2000, p. 64) inform us that the other members of the conference coalition on the Burger Court reacted to the initial draft of the majority opinion in the following ways:

1. Sent a memo to the majority opinion writer that indicated that they hereby join the majority opinion (79.4 percent of the time);

2. Sent a memo threatening not to join the majority opinion unless specific changes in the opinion were made (1.8 percent of the time);

3. Made suggestions for changes in the majority opinion (2.8 percent of the time);

4. Informed the majority opinion writer that they would decide whether to join after the other opinions are circulated (2.7 percent of the time);

5. Sent a memo to the majority opinion writer indicating that they would be writing a separate opinion (2.4 percent of the time);

6. Circulated or joined a concurring opinion (8 percent of the time); and

7. Circulated or joined a dissenting opinion (3 percent of the time).

To what extent did the justices who did not initially join the majority opinion do so eventually? Maltzman, Spriggs, and Wahlbeck (2000, pp. 91–92) supplied this information for the justices who reacted in the ways indicated by items 2–6. The relevant statistics are 41.8 percent, 58.2 percent, 33.8 percent, 19.8 percent, and 18.7 percent. They, however, do not tell us the extent to which the justices who circulated or joined a dissenting opinion in reaction to the initial draft of the majority opinion (i.e., item 7) eventually joined the majority opinion. Apparently Maltzman, Spriggs, and Wahlbeck assume that they never did so.

We will accept their assumption for the purposes of this analysis.[6]

Finally, we want to know whether the justices who did not initially join the majority opinion but did so eventually joined because the majority opinion writer altered the initial opinion to please them. In other words, they joined the majority opinion after successful bargaining with the majority opinion writer. Maltzman, Spriggs, and Wahlbeck (2000, p. 81) assume that all of them did so. Although we believe that this is an overstatement, we will make the same assumption when we calculate the extent of successful bargaining on the Court. We will do so because a conservative scientific approach is to test hypotheses based on assumptions suggested by the other side.

Based on these two assumptions and the information supplied by Maltzman, Spriggs, and Wahlbeck (2000), we discovered that successful bargaining took place in less than 6 percent of the situations on the Burger Court (see Table 8.1).

Why is it that more successful bargaining did not occur? Some members of the conference coalition probably did not seek any changes in the majority opinion because they viewed

---

[6] It is possible, however, that in one or two cases in a given term, a given justice first voted with the majority at the conference vote on the merits, then circulated or joined a dissenting opinion, and then shifted to the majority and joined the majority opinion.

Table 8.1. *Successful Bargaining over the Content of the Majority Opinion on the Burger Court*

Behavior	Initial Reaction by Other Justices in the Conference Coalition (%)	Justice Joins Majority Coalition (%)	Bargaining (%)
1) Join Majority Opinion	79.4	100	0
2) Threat	1.8	41.8	.75
3) Suggestion	2.8	58.2	1.63
4) Wait	2.7	33.8	.91
5) Will Write	2.4	19.8	.48
6) Circulate/Join Concurrence	8.0	18.7	1.50
7) Circulate/Join Dissent	3.0	0	0
TOTAL	100.1		5.26

Columns 1 and 2 were derived from Maltzman, Spriggs, and Wahlbeck (2000). This table ignores preemptive accommodation of the other members in the conference coalition or bargaining that may occur to induce the dissenting justices at the conference vote to shift to the majority and join the majority opinion.

the original majority opinion as good enough. In contrast, other members of the conference coalition probably did not seek any changes because they believed they had no hope that any bargaining with the majority opinion writer would result in a majority opinion that would be acceptable to them. This reaction is certainly true for those members of the conference coalition who no longer favored the outcome supported in the majority opinion and, therefore, circulated or joined a dissenting opinion. It might also be true for most of those justices who were unhappy with the rule of law or legal reasoning presented in that opinion and circulated or joined a concurring opinion, for these justices joined the majority opinion only 18.7 percent of the time. In short, successful bargaining took place only in the intermediate position.

This behavior is somewhat comparable to buying a house. In a seller's market, if the asking price is satisfactory and the buyer fears that someone else is also likely to make an offer during a given period, she may offer the asking price or even offer a slightly higher price and is likely to buy the house without bargaining with the owner. If, however, the buyer believes that the price is much too high, she probably will not make any offer at all. (Note that lowballing rarely works in a seller's market.) Only in the intermediate position will the buyer attempt to bargain with the owner and, of course, not all attempts will be successful.

The Extent of Successful Bargaining over the Content

This topic is important because successful bargaining over the content of the majority opinion is one of the clearest examples we have of strategic behavior on the Court. It is, therefore, of some interest that it probably takes place between the majority opinion writer and the other justices in the conference coalition in less than 6 percent of the situations.

The bargaining referred to in this chapter, however, somewhat underestimates the amount of strategic behavior in the drafting of the majority opinion, for there will be cases in which a certain amount of "preemptive accommodation" (Maltzman, Spriggs, and Wahlbeck, 2000, p. 98) will take place. In other words, the majority opinion writer will write the first draft of his opinion to reflect the views of one or more of the other justices in the conference coalition. Maltzman, Spriggs, and Wahlbeck (2000, p. 98) tell us, however, that

> ... Opinion authors are unlikely, and possibly unwise, to incorporate fully the preferences of their colleagues in the first draft.... Accommodating colleagues immediately may deplete an author's subsequent bargaining leverage....

> Even if opinion authors want to attract the support of their brethren with the first draft, justices ... do not have perfect information and may not know exactly which position will attract the support of which colleagues.

In addition, the bargaining referred to in this chapter does not include any bargaining involved to induce a justice who dissented at the conference vote to shift sides and join the majority opinion. We have argued, however (see Chapter 7), that such bargaining will rarely occur on the Court.

In short, based on the analysis presented previously, we believe that there is much less bargaining over the content of the majority opinion than some Supreme Court scholars assert.

A final comment: In this chapter, we have focused on how often *the individual justices* in the conference coalition successfully bargain with the majority opinion writer. Those scholars who seek to emphasize strategic behavior on the Court are likely to ask: How often does one or more of the justices in a given case successfully bargain with the majority opinion writer? Baum (1997, pp. 106–107), citing an unpublished and unavailable paper written by Sandra Woods, tells us that one or more of the justices on the Burger Court requested a change in the majority opinion in 33 percent of the cases and that the majority opinion writer accepted these changes in two thirds of the cases. Presumably, these justices, then, joined the majority opinion. Thus, in 22 percent of the cases on the Burger Court, one or more of the justices successfully bargained with the majority opinion writer.

Should we use the 22 percent statistic instead of the 6 percent statistic when talking about the extent of successful bargaining over the content of the majority opinion? To answer this question, it is useful to focus on the situation in which seven justices are members of the conference coalition, one successfully bargains with the majority opinion writer, and the other five send a memo to him indicating that they hereby join the initial opinion. One consequence of using the 22 percent statistic in this situation is that we end up ignoring the behavior of the other five justices. In contrast, when we use the 6 percent statistic we are using all the data.

CHAPTER NINE

The Size of Opinion Coalitions

Rohde (1972) viewed opinion coalition formation on the Court as a bargain between the majority opinion writer and the other justices on the Court wherein the majority opinion writer will alter her ideal opinion in exchange for the other justices' votes. Although the majority opinion writer will desire an opinion that reflects her ideal position, she would be willing to modify it to obtain sufficient additional votes for it so that her opinion will be an authoritative opinion of the Court (also known as a majority opinion), instead of a plurality opinion. Four votes will be needed if eight or nine justices are participating in the case. The majority opinion writer, however, would be unwilling to change her opinion after a minimum winning (MW) vote is secured, and the other justices will not join the opinion unless additional changes are made. As a consequence, opinion coalitions on the Supreme Court will be MW.

This MW model pertains only to nonthreat cases (i.e., to cases in which no outside group is threatening the Court). In threat cases, Rohde argued, the Court is likely to form a united front against the threat. In other words, some justices would be willing to vote against their ideological predispositions to protect the Court against the threat.

This model is based on a number of unrealistic assumptions. First, Rohde assumes that the majority opinion writer will seek an opinion that reflects her views. This is a reasonable assumption, but it is also possible that she will seek an opinion that mirrors the views of the members of the conference coalition (see Chapter 10). Second, Rohde assumes that a justice will not join the majority opinion unless it is altered to conform to his views. This assumption appears to be in conflict with the evidence we presented in Chapter 8, which indicates that almost 80 percent of the members of the conference coalition on the Burger Court reacted to the initial draft of the majority opinion by sending a memo that indicated that they hereby join the opinion. In other words, the opinion writer did not have to alter her opinion to pick up the votes of these justices. Third, Rohde assumes that the majority opinion writer will always be able to obtain four additional votes for her opinion, but, in a small percentage of cases, the Court hands down a plurality opinion. Fourth, he assumes that after a majority vote is secured for the opinion, the majority opinion writer will not be willing to change her opinion to pick up additional votes. Murphy (1964, pp. 65–66), however, tells us that

> [even after a majority vote is obtained for the opinion]...the marginal value of another vote is never zero, though the asking price may exceed its real value and may have to be rejected. In the judicial process a 5–4 decision emphasizes the strength of the losing side and may encourage resistance and evasion. The greater the majority, the greater the appearance of certainty and the more likely a decision will be accepted and following in similar cases.

Fifth, and most important, Rohde's model ignores the close relationship between the size of the conference coalition and the size of the opinion coalition. Finally, Rohde ignores the possibility that one or more of the dissenting justices at the conference vote might shift to the majority and join the majority opinion, even though his specific views have not been accommodated and the case in question does not involve a threat to the Court. A few of these points will be mentioned again in evaluating Rohde's empirical study.

Rohde inspected the civil liberties cases on the Warren Court and discovered that, in nonthreat cases, 40 percent of the opinion coalitions were five-member coalitions and 63 percent were five- or six-member coalitions. In threat cases, however, opinion coalitions tended to consist of eight or nine members or five or six members in about equal proportions. Rohde contended that the six-person opinion coalitions ought to be viewed as MW because the opinion writer, "uncertain about the behavior of the other members" and concerned about obtaining a majority vote for his opinion, might make "his policy broader than . . . necessary and thus [secure] the assent of more than the minimum number of justices" (Rohde, 1972, p. 213).

Should we be impressed with Rohde's nonthreat results of 40 percent and 63 percent? Most scholars were not (Baum, 1997, p. 105; Brenner, 2003). Brenner (1979b), for example, noted that the 40 percent and 63 percent statistics are less than the amounts of 49.2 percent and 82 percent that we would expect if the justices voted at random, hardly an impressive result for an MW theory. We believe that they should have been substantially higher than random because Rohde was investigating civil liberties cases on the Warren Court. In other words, he was examining cases that were often salient to the justices and, therefore, in which they would want to express their views. In addition, consensus norms were weak on the Warren Court, and, thus, the justices had the freedom to vote their preferences.

Brenner (1979b) inspected the 1946 to 1955 era of the Court and discovered that, instead of MW opinion coalitions, opinion coalitions tended to be either the same size as the conference vote or one or two votes larger. Indeed, even when a tentative MW coalition was in place at the conference vote (i.e., the conference coalition consisted of five or six justices), additional votes were obtained for the majority opinion 38 percent of the time.

Rohde's threat findings have been criticized as well. Brenner and Arrington (1980), for example, showed that the difference in the size of the opinion coalitions on the Warren Court is not associated with a comparison between threat cases and nonthreat cases, as defined by Rohde, but, rather, with a comparison between the racial discrimination cases and all the other civil liberties cases. Only regarding the racial discrimination cases did the Court form a united front. Perhaps only when the threat is severe will some of the justices be willing to vote against their policy or legal preferences and join the majority opinion.

If Rohde's analysis is not useful for determining the size of the opinion coalitions, what is? We suggest that one should examine the conditions under which the justices are likely to join the majority opinion (see Maltzman, Spriggs, and Wahlbeck, 2000, pp. 141–147). These three scholars examined this question for the Burger Court and discovered twelve conditions associated with membership in that opinion. Not surprisingly, one of these conditions is membership in the conference coalition. Based on these conditions, different size majority opinion coalitions can be expected under different conditions.

Note, however, that even though we do not find any support for Rohde's ambitious MW thesis, Maltzman, Spriggs, and Wahlbeck (2000, pp. 105–106) discovered that a majority opinion writer was less likely to alter his opinion to satisfy the other justices in the conference coalition after he obtained an MW vote for his opinion. Thus, a more modest MW thesis can be supported.

CHAPTER TEN

At Whose Ideal Point Will the Majority Opinion Be Written?

Although United States Supreme Court scholars have long recognized that the majority opinion constitutes "the core of the policy-making power of the Supreme Court" (Rohde and Spaeth, 1976, p. 172), only recently have a number of scholars systematically investigated the processes involved in the drafting of this opinion (e.g., Epstein and Knight, 1998; Maltzman, Spriggs, and Wahlbeck, 2000; Bonneau, Hammond, Maltzman, and Wahlbeck, 2007). But none of the recent research supplies us with a good answer to the question: At whose ideal point will the majority opinion be written? In their conclusion to their famous text, Segal and Spaeth (2002, pp. 434–435) list this question as one of the six questions that ought to be explored. And Westerland (2003, p. 2) maintains that this question is "arguably the most important outstanding question about what the Court does."

Why should Supreme Court scholars be interested in at whose ideal point the majority opinion will be written? The main reason is that answering this question will increase our understanding of (1) the content of the majority opinion, (2) coalition formation on the Court, (3) the goals of the majority opinion assigner and writer, and (4) the consequences of majority opinion assignment. Concerning the latter, if the majority opinion writer tends to write the opinion at her own ideal point or at a point close to it, which justice is assigned to write the opinion in a given case is of great importance, but which justice is assigned to author the majority opinion is not of great importance if the majority opinion writer tends to write the majority opinion either at the ideal point of the Court median or at the ideal point of the conference coalition median. As Lax and Cameron (2005, p. 2) tell us:

> It is not obvious that assignments *should* matter. For example, if bargaining inevitably drives the position of cases to the ideal point of the median voter [on the Court], it does not matter who writes the initial opinion and thus it does not matter who makes the assignment.... If the price of forming a majority coalition is always the same, why does it matter who writes the check?

The Majority Opinion Writer Hypothesis

We can suggest at least three ideal points at which the majority opinion might be written: the ideal point of the majority opinion writer, the ideal point of the median justice on the Court, and the ideal point of the median justice in the conference coalition. In this section, we present an argument for believing that the majority opinion will be written at the ideal point of the majority opinion writer.

Conventional wisdom suggests that the majority opinion will be written at the ideal point of the majority opinion writer (Epstein and Knight, 1998, p. 126; Maltzman and Wahlbeck, 2004, p. 552; Segal and Spaeth, 2002, p. 377; Ulmer, 1970, p. 51). Ulmer (1970, p. 51) offered the classical statement: "Each justice being unique, each opinion reflects, to some extent, the particular attributes of the writer – his conception of the law, his previous positions, his facility with language and concepts, and so on." The opinion assignment literature is usually based on this assumption. It is conventional, for example, to argue that in salient cases the majority opinion writers will either self-assign the majority opinion or assign it to an ideological ally (Maltzman and Wahlbeck, 2004, p. 552). This argument makes sense only if one believes that the majority opinion writer will hand down an opinion that mirrors his views or one close to them. Consistent with this argument, Maltzman, Spriggs, and Wahlbeck (2000, p. 70) contend that "the majority opinion author's overriding goal [is]: to produce an opinion that as closely as possible reflects his or her view of the case" (see also Maltzman, Spriggs, and Wahlbeck, 2000, p. 98).

If the majority opinion writer is seeking an opinion that mirrors her views or one close to it,[7] this goal is facilitated by her agenda-control powers. Maltzman, Spriggs, and Wahlbeck (2000, pp. 7 and 34) tell us that the majority opinion writer makes the "first move in the case." She "proposes a policy position from the range of available alternatives." The other justices "can seek changes in the drafts of the majority opinion." But "these are not designed to be competing policy alternatives but rather are intended to make existing opinion drafts more acceptable to the individual justice" (see also Epstein and Knight, 1998, pp. 126–127). As a consequence, the other justices, even when they join the majority opinion, will often tolerate an opinion that is less than ideal from their perspective.

One might ask: Why is it that the other justices in the conference coalition would be willing to join a majority opinion

---

[7] We refer to an opinion that is "close to it" because the majority opinion writer will want to pick up four additional votes and may have to alter her ideal opinion in order to do so. (See Chapter 9.)

when it is not ideal from their perspective? Bonneau and Hammond (2005, p. 30) supply three answers: (1) the other "justices understand that opinions not backed by a Court majority are not generally treated as precedent," (2) there is a "limit on each justice's time and resources . . . [that] might often preclude them from crafting an alternative to the draft majority opinion," and (3) there may be a "norm of reciprocity by which justices tacitly agree to give the majority author some discretion: A justice may give up something on one case but get something back on a case of greater interest."

We assume that if the majority opinion is written at a given justice's ideal point, she will be satisfied with it and will not write or join a regular or a special concurring opinion or a dissenting opinion. For our empirical tests, we want to determine how often the three candidate justices – the majority opinion writer, the median justice on the Court, and the median justice in the conference coalition – write or join such opinions, but because the majority opinion writer rarely or never writes a concurring or a dissenting opinion, we will focus, instead, on whether the justice in the conference coalition ideologically closest to her will write or join a concurring or a dissenting opinion.

We, now, turn to the argument that the majority opinion will be written at the ideal point of the median justice on the Court.

The Court Median Hypothesis

A major challenge to the conventional wisdom comes from some scholars who view decision making on the Supreme Court as similar to decision making in two-party elections. The median voter theorem (Black, 1958; Downs, 1957) suggests that, in elections involving two rival political parties in which the voters are deciding how to vote based on a single dimension (typically liberalism vs. conservatism), both parties will move their platforms to the center to attract the vote of the median voter in the electorate and, thereby, win the election. Applying this model, Spiller (2000, p. 943) tells us that

> The only agenda power of the chief justice (or the senior justice in the majority) is the assignment of who will write the opinion, but... other justices make all sorts of suggestions (proposals) through memoranda, conversations, and concurrences. In principle, then, the agenda power in the Court is minimal at best. When issues are single dimensional, a majority should not be that hard to form, in principle, and should include the 'median' justice on that dimension.... Indeed, unless it is expensive to write an opinion,... the final opinion could not differ from the median justice's preferred opinion. If there is any difference with her preferred outcome, she would write such an opinion and garner a majority.

[92]

This quotation suggests that the median voter theorem is even more likely to work in the context of Supreme Court decision making than in the context of two-party elections because the median justice on the Court can play an active role in ensuring that the opinion will be written at her ideal point.

There are a number of reasons to doubt this logic, however. We will mention three of them. First, the proponents of the Court median hypothesis underestimate the majority opinion writer's agenda-control powers.

Second, the advocates of this hypothesis underestimate the costs involved in negotiating with the majority opinion writer and in drafting alternative opinions.

Third, the champions of the Court median hypothesis ignore the fact that the median justice on the Court, if she is a member of the conference coalition, is likely to remain in that coalition at the final vote (Dorff and Brenner, 1992). The median justice is particularly likely to remain in the coalition when the conference vote is 6–3, 7–2, 8–1, or 9–0, in other words, when justices less committed to the ideological position favored by the Court at the conference vote also voted for that position. But the median justice is also likely to remain in the coalition when the conference coalition is MW. As Westerland (2003, 14) argues:

[93]

> Because the justices vote on the merits of the case before writing the opinion, it may be very difficult for dissenters to entice potential swing votes.... For minority justices to entice the median member of the Court after a 5–4 vote, they must convince the median to change her vote.... [But] the difference between the dissenters and the closest member of the majority coalition could be insurmountable. If the median sincerely believes a lower court decision should be affirmed and the dissenters sincerely believe that it should be reversed, it is hard to imagine a counteroffer from the dissenters that is preferable to *any* offer from the majority coalition.

The majority opinion writer is likely to be aware of the fact that the median justice on the Court is likely to remain in the coalition and, therefore, will be under little or no pressure to write the opinion at her ideal point.

One can imagine, of course, a given median justice on the Court, who is a member of an MW conference coalition, threatening to shift to the other side unless the majority opinion writer agrees to write his opinion at her ideal point (see Murphy, Pritchett, Epstein, and Knight, 2006, p. 636). But how often can the median justice play this game? If the median justice does not actually favor the outcome on the other side, the majority opinion writer might recognize that she is bluffing and call her bluff. He might even ignore her threat when she is seriously considering shifting to the other side. A median justice's prior behavior is likely to influence the reaction of the majority opinion writer, but despite the discussion in this paragraph, one should not assume that decision making on the Court is similar to as decision making in poker. Bluffing in poker is legitimate and an essential part of the game. Bluffing in Supreme Court decision making is likely to be perceived by the other justices as insincere and illegitimate.

One can also imagine that a given median justice on the Court, who is a member of an MW conference coalition, threatens to write a special concurring opinion unless the majority opinion writer agrees to write his opinion at her ideal point. But if the majority opinion writer so agrees, he risks the possibility that the extreme justice in the conference coalition will write a special concurring opinion. We suspect that neither of these two justices will threaten to write special concurring opinions very often.

Spiller, of course, assumes that if the majority opinion writer refuses to write the opinion at the median justice's ideal point, the median justice will take over and use her median position on the Court to obtain four votes for her ideal opinion. We do not understand whose votes the median justice on the Court will be able to attract, because justices who dissented at the conference coalition are hardly likely to be good candidates to support an opinion favored by the median

[95]

justice on the Court who voted for the opposite outcome at the conference vote. Only if one assumes that the median justice on the Court is equally likely to vote for either outcome, despite having voted one way or the other at the conference vote (with the other justices voting 4–4), will the median justice on the Court be in a good strategic position to control the content of the majority opinion, but this situation will seldom occur on the Court. Note that the median justice on the Court could be uncertain which outcome to favor prior to the conference vote. After this vote takes place, however, the median justice on the Court has announced her vote for a specific outcome and is unlikely to change.

These reasons suggest to us that there is no reason to believe that the majority opinion will be written at the ideal position of the median justice on the Court.

The Conference Coalition Median Hypothesis

Although the median voter theorem, as we have argued, is probably not applicable to the Court as a whole, it could be applicable to the conference coalition. Whether it is applicable or not to the conference coalition depends on whether the assumptions underlying this hypothesis are reasonable. We can suggest three assumptions: (1) that the other members of the conference coalition are likely to remain in the conference coalition and join the majority opinion; (2) that the majority opinion writer will want to, or be compelled to, write an opinion that is likely to appeal to all the members of the winning coalition and not write one that appeals to the dissenters at that vote; and (3) that the best way for her to do so is for her to write the opinion at the ideal point of the median justice in the conference coalition.

The first assumption is clearly reasonable. Maltzman and Wahlbeck (1996, p. 588) discovered that only 4.6 percent of the members of the conference coalition on the Burger Court shifted to the other side. Maltzman, Spriggs, and Wahlbeck (2000) indicate that almost 85 percent of the other members of the conference coalition on the Burger Court either initially joined the majority opinion (79.4 percent) or joined it after successful bargaining over the content of the majority opinion (5.26 percent) (see Chapter 8).

Maltzman, Spriggs, and Wahlbeck (2000, pp. 96–97) tell us, regarding the second assumption, that

> ... if [the] opinion authors know that their colleagues are unlikely to sign an opinion that does not reflect their preferences, [the] authors may try to write an opinion comporting with the discussion of the case at conference and thus satisfy their brethren with the first draft of an opinion. We term this type of behavior *preemptive accommodation....*

Additional anecdotal evidence of preemptive accommodation abounds. According to Chief Justice Rehnquist,
the purpose of the conference discussion is to determine
the views of the majority of the Court, thus allowing the
author to write an opinion reflecting their views....
Justice Lewis Powell, moreover, instructed his new clerk:
'When I am writing in a case...the conference views of
other justices on the issue presented...must be taken
into account...' Opinion authors, in short, realize that,
in developing the first draft of an opinion, they are con-
strained by their colleagues' preferences as stated at conference.

Maltzman, Spriggs, and Wahlbeck (2000, p. 70) also
inform us that after the first draft of the majority opinion
is circulated, the majority opinion writer will often respond
favorably to the suggestions for change made by the members
of the conference coalition (see Chapter 8).

In contrast, the majority opinion writer will rarely receive
suggestions for change in the opinion from the justices
who dissented at the conference vote, and if she receives
such suggestions she will usually ignore them (Maltzman,
Spriggs, and Wahlbeck, 2000, pp. 70–72). The dissenting justices, at times, will shift to the other side (Maltzman and
Wahlbeck, 1996) and even join the majority opinion, but there
is no reason to believe that they will obtain any benefit from
the majority opinion writer when they do. Based upon this

evidence, the second assumption appears to be reasonable as well.

The third assumption, that the best way for the majority opinion writer to write an opinion that appeals to all the members of the winning coalition is to write it at the ideal point of the median justice in the conference coalition, is based on the underlying assumption that the closer the opinion is to an individual justice's ideal point, the more likely this justice will find it appealing. If the opinion is not written at the ideal point of the median justice in the conference coalition, the median justice (or any other justice in the conference coalition) has an incentive to draft an alternative opinion written at this ideal point and such an opinion is more likely to attract the support of the justices in the conference coalition than the majority opinion. Note that the author of this alternative opinion is seeking the support of justices who favor the same outcome as he does.

Hypotheses

In this chapter we have advanced an argument for the position that the majority opinion writer will write the opinion at his ideal point or close to it as well as an argument that he will write it at the ideal point of the median justice in the conference coalition. Both of these arguments are based on the material in Maltzman, Spriggs, and Wahlbeck (2000). In fact, these three scholars (2000, p. 9) state that "an opinion author is likely... to try to draft an opinion that reflects both his or her own policy goal and the preferences of the expected majority coalition."

Which of these two goals is more important? Brenner and Whitmeyer (ND) attempted to answer this question. Indeed, they tested all three possible alternatives:

Hypothesis 1. The opinion will be written at the ideal point of the median justice *in the conference coalition* and, as a consequence, he is less likely to write or join a concurring or a dissenting opinion.

Hypothesis 2. The opinion will be written at the ideal point of the majority opinion writer and, as a consequence, the justice ideologically closest to her is less likely to write or join a concurring or a dissenting opinion.

Hypothesis 3. The opinion will be written at the ideal point of the median justice *on the Court* when that justice is a member of the conference coalition and, as a consequence, this justice is less likely to write or join a concurring or a dissenting opinion.

Findings

Brenner and Whitmeyer (ND) examined the data from the Vinson, Warren, and Burger Courts and discovered that the median justice *in the conference coalition* was less likely to write a concurring or a dissenting opinion than the other two justices designated in Hypotheses 2 and 3. This was particularly true in salient cases, in other words, in cases in which the other justices in the conference coalition cared a great deal about the content of the majority opinion. We, of course, are not surprised that the median justice *on the Court,* when a member of the conference coalition, was more likely to write a dissenting or a concurring opinion, but why was the justice ideologically closest to the majority opinion writer more likely to write a dissenting or a concurring opinion?

In a typical situation, all members of the conference coalition will be satisfied with the majority opinion, and none of these justices will write or join a concurring or a dissenting opinion. Maltzman, Spriggs, and Wahlbeck (2000) tell us that on the Burger Court 79 percent of the members of the conference coalition reacted to the initial draft of the majority opinion by sending a memo to the majority opinion writer that he hereby joins it (see Chapter 8). Of course, one can join the majority opinion and also write or join a regular concurring opinion. In other situations, one or more justices will not be satisfied with it, but because the majority opinion writer himself is a middle justice in the conference coalition, the dissatisfied justices will not include either the median justice in the conference coalition or the justice ideologically closest to the majority opinion writer. Consider, however, the situation in which the majority opinion writer is B in a conference coalition of ABCDEFG and A is the justice ideologically closest to him. If the majority opinion writer is attempting to write an opinion that appeals to either all members of the conference coalition or at least picks up four additional votes, it makes sense for him to write an opinion that pleases D more than A. The same argument can be made when F is the majority opinion writer and G is ideologically closest to him. Similar arguments can be made when the conference coalition consists of ABCDE or EFGHI or is unanimous.

In short, if a primary goal of the majority opinion writer is to retain the votes of the members of the conference coalition, in some situations it makes more sense for the majority opinion writer to move the opinion to where most of the justices in the conference coalition are located than to move it toward an ideologically closest justice who is located in the opposite direction.

CHAPTER ELEVEN

Reciprocity on the Supreme Court

Do the justices exchange votes or join each other's opinions? In groups like the United States Supreme Court – that are small and repeatedly engage in collective decision making – such an exchange is likely to be a beneficial strategy for all the actors. It certainly could make sense for the Supreme Court justices. Suppose that, contrary to her personal preferences, Justice A votes with other justices on some cases about which she cares less, and the other justices vote with her on some cases about which they care less. All the justices ought to end up more satisfied. Such an exchange, however, will violate the ideal of justice, according to which the outcome of each case ought to depend on its own merits. The justices who aspire to this ideal, therefore, may refuse to engage in such an exchange. In this regard, Justice Breyer (Toobin, 2005) stated:

> Tomorrow is another day. No dependency of a decision of one case on another. You join me, I join you. None of that. None of that, zero. The coalitions float. Each one, one case, is a new day. Each day is a new day.

We agree that justices do not exchange votes on cases in such a way as to affect the decisions in the cases, but the justices still may join one another's opinions reciprocally or they may leave minorities and join majorities reciprocally. We focus on these two possibilities in the remainder of this chapter.

The Theory of Exchange

Complicating this question of reciprocity is that there are many kinds of possible exchanges in Supreme Court decision making. Small groups researchers have distinguished between different kinds of exchange based on who is giving to whom, who is reciprocating, and how the exchange is arranged (see Ekeh, 1974; Molm, 1997; Yamagishi and Cook, 1993). Two kinds of exchange possible in the Supreme Court are dyadic (or two-person) exchanges and group-focused group-generalized exchanges. A dyadic exchange is straight-forward: Justice A, for example, joins Justice B's opinion in some case in return for Justice B's joining his opinion in another case. Alternatively, Justice A can vote for the out-come favored by Justice B in one case in exchange for Justice B voting for his preferred outcome in another case.

A dyadic exchange is simple to understand. Microeconomic theory supports the idea that two actors are likely to engage in an exchange if both will be better off after the exchange than before. Two justices should exchange, therefore – vote with the other or join the other's opinions – if each will be better off by doing so.

A group-focused group-generalized exchange takes place, for example, when Justice A is a lone dissenter in an 8–1 conference vote. Hoping for future reciprocity, Justice A joins the other justices for the final vote. Subsequently, on a case when a different justice, say Justice D, finds himself the lone dissenter at the conference vote, he joins the majority at the final vote, returning the earlier favor of Justice A.

A group-focused group-generalized exchange is more complicated because built into the exchange is a free-rider problem. Let us examine the above example. Justice D was in the majority at the conference vote. He and his colleagues would like the minority justices, here only Justice A, to join and vote with the majority at the final vote. Justice A should be inclined to do so if it constitutes reciprocity, that is, if the conference coalition justices (B through I) tend to join Justice A's coalition when they are in the minority and she is in the conference coalition.

The problem, however, is that each justice is tempted to vote her own preferences and not reciprocate, relying on her partners in majority coalitions to reciprocate and, thus, keep reciprocity alive. For example, when Justice A is in the minority and considering whether to switch her vote she may think, "If I join the others' coalition on this case, then they will be more likely to join my majority coalition on later cases." But she may also think, "Suppose I do not join the majority this time. Suppose in some future case, Justice D is in the minority at the conference vote and I am in the majority. As long as my other partners in the conference coalition have joined Justice D when he has been in the majority, he is still likely to join us out of reciprocity. I need not be cooperative, therefore, for as long as the other justices are cooperative I shall be fine." The threat to cooperation, of course, is that if too many justices reason that way, there will not be enough reciprocity to make it worthwhile for any justice to reciprocate, and reciprocity and cooperation will disappear entirely.

Experimental work on group-focused group-generalized exchange has supported this reasoning (e.g., Yamagishi and Cook, 1993). In this situation, assuming that all actors would be better off under total cooperation than under total non-cooperation, two equilibria are possible. One is a cooperative equilibrium, in which all group members cooperate and reciprocate at a high level, and the other is a noncooperative equilibrium in which no group members cooperate and reciprocate. Often it is a matter of initial levels of cooperation. If cooperation and reciprocity start out high in a group, the levels tend to stay high or rise even higher, to nearly full cooperation: The group is attracted to the high-reciprocity equilibrium. If the initial level of cooperation is too low, however, then cooperation tends to drop to nothing: The group is attracted to the low-reciprocity equilibrium. This kind of behavior contrasts with dyadic exchange, in which cooperation and reciprocity is the predicted outcome as long as cooperation is better than noncooperation for both.

Empirical Evidence in the Supreme Court

How much dyadic exchange is there on the Court? Arrington and Brenner (2008) examined minimum winning opinion coalitions at the conference vote on the Vinson, Warren, and Burger Courts and found no evidence that the opinion writer attracts more votes for his opinions if he had previously joined other justices' majority opinions.

But do pairs of justices join each other's concurring and dissenting opinions? Westerland (2004) conducted the best study on this topic. He inspected the 1953 to 2000 era and discovered that cooperation between pairs of justices only took place between ideological allies (p. 11), but even these justices "generally do not join one another's non-majority opinions" (p. 18). Also, when a justice joins a colleague's nonmajority opinions a certain percentage of the time, the other justice rarely reciprocates at or near the same level. In short, "most justices most of the time simply do not cooperate" (p. 11).

Theoretically this failure to cooperate is typically explained by assuming that the two actors would not be better off by an exchange. In other words, the two actors do not sufficiently value the outcome of a potential exchange. This explanation makes sense to us. What justices primarily care about is seeing their preferred outcome adopted by the Court. If their position is not adopted by the Court, they may want to express their views in a concurring or dissenting opinion, but it probably does them little good to have another justice sign onto their concurring or dissenting opinion.

On the Supreme Court, a group-focused group-generalized exchange will be manifested as an increase in the size of the majority from the conference vote to the final vote. Justices who voted with the minority at the conference coalition will join the majority at the final vote. Theoretically, we expect that the Court will tend to be attracted to either a high-reciprocity equilibrium or a low-reciprocity equilibrium. In other words, either almost all decisions will be unanimous, regardless of the conference vote, or few cases that were not unanimous at the conference vote will end up unanimous.

In fact, this pattern is precisely what the record shows. For much of the Supreme Court's history, including all of the 19th century and more than a third of the 20th century, almost all decisions were unanimous at the final vote or nearly so. This pattern may have appeared because John Marshall exerted strong pressure on the other justices to reach a consensus, and after the Court established that high-reciprocity equilibrium the equilibrium perpetuated itself just as experiments suggest. Starting with the Stone Court (1941–1946), however, dissents and concurrences at the final vote became increasingly frequent, so that there was little if any tendency for decisions that were not unanimous at the conference vote to move toward unanimity. In other words, for some historical reason, cooperation declined enough for the Court to become attracted to the low-reciprocity equilibrium rather than the high-reciprocity equilibrium.

Table 11.1 shows this historical change. It presents the proportions of decisions that were unanimous at the final vote at 10-year intervals from 1900 through the present, except for the crucial years in the 1940s when it gives the yearly

Table 11.1. *Unanimous Decisions of the U.S. Supreme Court, 1900–2004 Terms (Adapted from Epstein, Segal, Spaeth, and Walker (2007), Table 3–1)*

	1900–2004			1940s	
Year	*Proportion* *Unanimous*	*Court*	Year	*Proportion* *Unanimous*	*Court*
1900	.766	Fuller	1941	.609	Stone
1910	.893	White	1942	.490	Stone
1920	.820	White	1943	.385	Stone
1930	.892	Hughes	1944	.397	Stone
1940	.715	Hughes	1945	.425	Stone
1950	.371	Vinson	1946	.400	Vinson
1960	.320	Warren	1947	.316	Vinson
1970	.347	Burger	1948	.281	Vinson
1980	.352	Burger	1949	.376	Vinson
1990	.386	Rehnquist			
2000	.450	Rehnquist			
2004	.368	Rehnquist			

proportion. Especially striking is the speed with which the high-reciprocity equilibrium collapsed. From .715 in 1940 it dropped below .4 by 1943 and never again rose above .45.

Reciprocity is not the only reason, of course, for the Supreme Court to have high levels of unanimity. Some scholars speak of a "consensus norm" that existed. A consensus norm is not an explanation, however, but simply a label for the observed pattern: If the Court tends to produce consensus at the final vote regardless of how it voted at the conference vote, we say there is a consensus norm. The question is why it exists. Attraction to a high-reciprocity equilibrium, as described previously, is a possible explanation. It could be, however, that in the past the justices thought it was their duty to vote with the majority at the final vote, or they may have been motivated to be helpful, without expecting anything in return. There may have been attempts to enforce consensus voting. The chief justice, for example, may have assigned fewer majority opinions to noncooperative justices. Other justices may have exerted social pressure, for example, by shunning those justices who did not cooperate and join the majority at the final vote.

We contend, however, that the empirical pattern of either a great deal of consensus or else almost none at the final vote would be expected if consensus voting were caused by reciprocity.

As a final point, we note that this sort of reciprocity and cooperation, to *augment* a majority, is apparently legitimate. This behavior contrasts with vote trading to *obtain* a majority. The latter affects which litigant wins at the final vote and, thus, violates the ideal, noted at the beginning of this chapter, that the outcome of each case should depend on its own merits. Increasing the size of the majority does not change who wins at the final vote, but simply makes the Court's voice appear clearer and less likely to be transitory. That this reciprocity is legitimate is shown by fact that Chief Justice Roberts explicitly advocated it in an interview he gave after the completion of his first term on the Court. He stated that he had the goal of increasing the amount of consensus on the Court, and argued that his colleagues should all benefit from the practice of joining each other's majority coalitions (Rosen, 2006). Our analysis suggests that, unless he can get the justices to adopt reciprocity as a practice almost all the time, he is unlikely to increase the levels of consensus much at all.

Part V

The Final Vote on the Merits

CHAPTER TWELVE

The Separation of Powers Model

In Chapters 5 through 11 we investigated intracourt strategies, in other words, strategies that a justice might pursue in light of how his colleagues on the Court were likely to behave. In this chapter and in Chapter 13 we will explore strategies that a justice might follow based on how outside audiences are likely to behave.

One of the Supreme Court's most important jobs is the interpretation of federal statutes. At times, it decides whether a federal statute is unconstitutional or not. More often, it merely decides what a statute means. In other words, we can distinguish between the Court's constitutional decisions and its statutory decisions. When the Court hands down a statutory decision, Congress, in turn, can enact an overriding statute. In response, the Court may have the opportunity of interpreting the new statute. The process, of course, can go on indefinitely, with neither institution having the last licks.

The separation of powers (SOP) model mainly focuses on the statutory decisions of the Court. Baum (2007, p. 147) describes this model:

> ... justices might try to calculate whether their preferred interpretation of a statute would be sufficiently unpopular in Congress to produce an override. If so, justices would modify their interpretations to avoid that result. By making implicit this compromise with Congress, the justices could get the best possible result under the circumstances: not the interpretation of a statute that they favor most, but one that is closer to their preferences than the new statute that Congress would enact to override the Court's decision.

Note that the advocates of the SOP model assume that the ultimate goal of the justices is to achieve a policy as close to their ideological preferences as possible and that they will take the possibility of a congressional override into consideration only inasmuch as it might prevent the achievement of this goal.

Segal and Spaeth (2002, pp. 106–110), however, argue that the justices are highly unlikely to be influenced by this model. They contend that

1. The SOP model is based on the assumption "that the justices have perfect and complete information about the preferences of Congress" but the justices do not have such information (p. 106).

2. If the justices believe that Congress is likely to enact an overriding statute, it often "can opt out of [the] statutory mode" and find a constitutional basis for its decision (p. 106).[8]

3. If the justices believe that Congress is likely to enact an overriding statute, it can manipulate the issue in the case and protect itself from a congressional override (p. 107).

4. The SOP model is based on the assumption that it is costless for Congress to adopt an overriding statute (p. 107) and, of course, this is not true.

5. It is difficult for Congress to enact an overriding statute because a number of members of Congress and the president have veto power (pp. 107–108).

6. Even if Congress passes an overriding statute, the Court is likely to have the opportunity of interpreting the new statute and fixing any problem caused by it (pp. 108–109).

---

[8] The behaviors in this point and the following one are strategic but do not conform to the SOP model.

7. Usually both branches of Congress and the president are not to the right or left of most justices appointed to the Court and this might be required for an overriding statute to be enacted (pp. 109–110).

The Number of Overriding Statutes

Whether the SOP model motivates the justices' behavior might be explored, at least initially, by focusing on the number of overriding statutes. If the number is large, it might suggest either that the justices were not trying to follow an SOP strategy or that they were trying to do so, but were ineffective in preventing overrides. If, in contrast, the number of overriding statutes is small, it might suggest either that Congress ignores the Court's decisions or that it tends to be satisfied with them. Congress could be satisfied with the Court's interpretation of the statutes either because the Court has followed the SOP strategy or because the Court agrees with Congress without having to follow this strategy.

Unfortunately, it is difficult to know even approximately the location of the threshold between a small number of overriding statutes (or anything else) and a large number. Hausegger and Baum (1999) tell us that in the 1978 to 1989 era Congress overrode a statutory decision entirely or in large part at least 5.6 percent of the time. Hettinger and Zorn (2005, p. 8) inform us that in an early study regarding labor and antitrust decision only 12 percent of the Court's statutory decisions provoked a congressional response. Yet, Baum and Hausegger (2004, p. 111) consider the 5.6 percent as high (2004, p. 111), whereas Hettinger and Zorn (2005, p. 8) treat the number of overriding statutes as "relatively rare." Fortunately, there are other ways of investigating the SOP model.

Testing the SOP Model

The SOP model involves the strategic interplay between two institutions: the Supreme Court and the Congress. Empirical investigations of this model concentrate on the behavior of one or the other. They ask either whether the justices shape their decision making according to their situation vis-à-vis Congress or key congressional players, or whether congressional overrides can be explained in part by the ideological position of the Congress or its key members relative to that of the Court. We believe that the studies of the justices' behavior are more relevant for understanding its strategic behavior and, therefore, we will look at these first.

The justices could follow the SOP strategy by modifying the content of the majority opinion, by voting for an outcome that is contrary to their preferred position, or both. If they simply modified the content of the majority opinion, it would be difficult to test because we usually lack data regarding the Court's preferred statutory interpretation and, therefore, will not know whether the Court did not adhere to it in its majority opinion. Thus, the SOP studies that interest us assume that, to avoid an overriding statute, the justices are willing to vote for a different outcome than the one they can be expected to prefer. We note, however, that implicitly these studies assume that the justices are also adjusting the content of the majority opinion because the Court cannot vote for a different outcome without also changing the content of the majority opinion.

We will explore two such studies. First, Segal and Spaeth (2002, pp. 341–346) examined the individual justices' voting in the 1946 to 1993 era and discovered that the justices' scores in the nonunanimous civil liberties *statutory* cases were similar to their scores in the nonunanimous civil liberties *constitutional* cases and did not change as the political environment in Congress and in the presidency changed. Segal and Spaeth believe that the justices' scores in both kinds of cases are consistent with the attitudinal model.

Second, Hansford and Damore (2000, p. 194) wondered whether an earlier version of the Segal and Spaeth study (namely, Segal, 1997) overlooked "strategic behavior occurring at a finer level of analysis." These two scholars inspected the orally argued statutory decisions in the 1963 to 1995 era and discovered that when both chambers of Congress and the president were more conservative than a given justice, the justice was more likely to vote in a conservative direction (p. 501). Hansford and Damore measured the ideology of the justices by examining their lifetime voting in constitutional cases in 13 issue areas.

Hansford and Damore (2000, p. 501) also discovered that when both chambers of Congress and the president were more liberal than a given justices *and* when there was an increasing number of recent overrides in the relevant issue area, the justice in question was more likely to vote in a liberal direction. Four other hypotheses based on the SOP model, however, were not supported. In light of these mixed findings, Hansford and Damore (2000, p. 505) concluded that

> ... there appear to be situations in which Supreme Court justices act as if they are somewhat constrained by Congress. Nevertheless, our theoretical model receives less than full empirical support, and it seems safe to conclude that much of the time the justices are relatively unconstrained by the preferences of Congress.

In contrast to the above analysis, Maltzman, Spriggs, and Wahlbeck (1999, p. 51) tell us that "individual case studies have shown that on highly salient issues there is some evidence of justices playing a separation of powers game" and, then, cite three cases in which they claim this apparently happened.[9] Murphy, Pritchett, Epstein, and Knight (2006, p. 339) inform us that scholars are divided regarding whether the justices follow the SOP model. In support of this model, they argue that the scholars "provide data that presumably 'conservative' courts *occasionally* reach 'liberal' rulings when liberals control the various elected institutions of government." (Emphasis supplied by us.) We do not deny that in some cases the justices vote in accord with the SOP model, but we agree with Baum (2006, pp. 72–77), who argues that the justices do not "routinely" behave in this way.

Some scholars argue that the SOP model is also applicable to *constitutional* decisions of the Court. Baum (2006, p. 76) tells us that "Congress could enact new statutes to limit or nullify the impact of these decisions as well," but he concludes that there is no reason to believe that the justices "routinely" adjust their *constitutional* decisions to avoid a congressional override.

---

[9] One of the cases they cite is *Marbury v Madison 1 Cranch* 137 (1803). In this case, Chief Justice Marshall undoubtedly behaved strategically, but the Court did not alter its outcome because of an act of Congress. Rather, it declared that act unconstitutional. In short, this is hardly a good example of the Court following the SOP model.

We now turn from studies of the justices' behavior to studies of congressional overrides. Such studies can provide indirect indications of whether the SOP considerations affect the justices' decisions and also can tell us whether it makes sense that they should. Baum and Hausegger (2004, pp. 113–115) inform us that Congress is more likely to enact an overriding statute when there is a large number of amicus briefs in opposition to the Court's decision on the merits and is less likely to do so when the Court's decision is unanimous. They also tell us that a large percentage of the overriding statutes are "relatively minor provisions of [broader] legislation" (p. 114) and the fact that they are overriding a decision of the Court is usually not mentioned in the committee reports or in the floor debates. In short, these overriding statutes are hardly involved in a conflict between the Court and Congress. Finally, Baum and Hausegger point out that some overrides take place after invitations by the Court to do so.

Hettinger and Zorn (2005) examine the effect of ideological congruence between the Court and key congressional players on congressional overrides in the 1967 to 1989 era. Their study is more sophisticated than many of the previous studies, for the authors use a method that allows them to separate the effects on the incidence of overrides from the effects on the timing of overrides. They also control for a number of other case characteristics known or believed to affect the occurrence of overrides, including the number of amicus briefs, involvement of the U.S. government on the losing side, and whether the decision was unanimous.

Hettinger and Zorn's (2005) key finding is that ideological congruence has no effect on the incidence or timing of congressional overrides. More overrides do not occur, nor do they occur more quickly, when the Court and key congressional players are farther apart ideologically. What are the implications of this key finding for the SOP model from the perspective of the justices? The absence of an effect could mean that the justices are following the SOP model perfectly. They adjust their decisions exactly right so that a Congress that is further from them ideologically is still not motivated to override their decisions. This conclusion, however, is scarcely credible. What is more credible, and what Hettinger and Zorn (2005, pp. 20–21) argue, is that "Congress pays little or no systematic attention to the ideological content of the Court's decisions in choosing which cases to address through legislation." This, in turn, suggests that the Court is unlikely to be motivated to follow the SOP model, for there is no point in trying to adjust decisions to conform ideologically to Congress to forestall overrides when ideological considerations generally do not affect overrides.

In short, we accept Baum's conclusion that following the SOP strategy is not standard practice for the justices. Empirical studies of the justices' behavior do not turn up any widespread use of this strategy. In addition, Congress's apparent obliviousness to ideological differences with the Court makes this strategy pointless.

CHAPTER THIRTEEN

Supreme Court Decision Making and Public Opinion

In most cases decided by the Court, the general public does not know that the Supreme Court has decided the case and, if they did know, would not have an opinion whether the case was decided correctly or not. In this chapter, however, we are interested in cases in which the general public knows that the Court has decided the case and has an opinion regarding that decision.

More specifically, we will attempt to answer two questions. First, do the justices attempt to avoid handing down individual decisions that are likely to be perceived negatively by the general public? Second, is the Court likely to be influenced by the "public mood?"

A justice, concerned with the possible negative reaction by the general public to a given decision, might ask herself the following questions: (1) Is it likely that the general public will react negatively to a given possible decision? (2) If it reacts negatively, will such reaction result in a loss of support for the Court? (3) If the general public is less supportive of the Court because of its negative reaction to a given possible decision, will that affect the Court's effectiveness? and (4) If it affects the Court's effectiveness, am I better off deciding the case based on my preferences or should I avoid handing down the decision to avoid the harm? Our reading of Baum (2006, p. 17) influenced our formulation of these four questions.

Baum (2006, p. 65) concluded that a justice will usually ignore a possible negative public reaction in deciding how to vote in a given case. We agree. Let us examine the four points mentioned above. The general public usually will react negatively to only a few decisions in a given Court, and it may be somewhat difficult for a Supreme Court justice to predict whether a given possible decision will fall into this category. Second, negative reaction to a given decision is unlikely to translate into a loss of support for the Court, particularly in the long run. This lack of a negative reaction may be true even regarding *Bush v Gore* 531 US 98 (2000) (see Gibson, Caldiera, and Spencer, 2003), even though this case decided the presidential election of 2000 and it was justified on the basis of a poorly reasoned majority opinion. Third, even if there is a loss of support for the Court, this is unlikely to result in a loss of the Court's effectiveness, unless the particular decision requires the general public or at least part of it to comply with the Court's decision or unless the public's loss of support influences congressional or executive action. Finally, a justice is much more likely to be concerned about pursuing her policy or legal goals than about whether some possible future harm will come to the Court, a harm that may never occur.

The Supreme Court, in addition, was established by the framers to be independent of public opinion. Justice Jackson, in *West Virginia State Board of Education v Barnette* 319 US 624 (1943), for example, tells us that

> The very purpose of the Bill of Rights was to withdraw certain subjects from the vicissitudes of political controversy, to place them beyond the reach of majorities and officials and to establish them as legal principles to be applied by the courts. One's right to life, liberty and property, to free speech, a free press, freedom of worship and assembly, and other fundamental rights may not be submitted to vote; they depend on the outcome of no elections.

In pursuance of this philosophy, the Court has upheld minority rights, even when a majority of public opinion favored the other side. This disregard of public opinion was particularly true during the Warren Court (1953 term through the 1968 term). There were a host of landmark decisions in that Court that were contrary to public opinion or, at least a significant segment of public opinion. Consider the following decisions of the Warren Court:

1. *Brown v Board of Education* 347 US 483 (1954), in which the Court held that "separate but equal" public schools in the various states violated the Equal Protection clause of the Fourteenth Amendment of the U.S. Constitution, and *Bolling v Sharpe* 347 US 335 (1954), in which the Court held that "separate but equal" schools in Washington, D.C., violated the Due Process clause of the Fifth Amendment.

2. *Engel v Vitale* 370 US 421 (1962), in which the Supreme Court held that it is a violation of the Establishment clause of the First Amendment for public school officials to require or to allow pupils to recite a state-composed, denominationally neutral prayer at the beginning of the school day. In the following year the Court in *Abington v Schempp* and *Murray v Curlett* 374 US 203 (1963) held that the state-ordered recitation of the Lord's Prayer from the New Testament and the reading of the King James' version of the Bible in the public schools are also prohibited by the Establishment clause. Note that a majority of the population have never supported *Abington and*

Murray (see Epstein, Segal, Spaeth, and Walker, 2007, Table 8-26).

3.   Numerous decisions of the 1950s that upheld the free speech and other constitutional rights of communists and other leftists. These decisions took place during a time when the American people were afraid of Communist spies and subversives. The Warren Court, however, after being threatened by Congress, retreated from this position in such cases as *Barenblatt v United States* 360 US 109 (1959) and *Communist Party v Subversive Activities Control Board* 367 US 1 (1961).

4.   Numerous decisions that favored the rights of criminal defendants. One of the most dramatic of these decisions was *Miranda v Arizona* 384 US 436 (1966), in which the Supreme Court held that suspects in police custody have a constitutional right to be informed that they have a right to remain silent, that anything they say may be used against them in court, that they have the right to consult an attorney, that they have the right to have their attorney present during questioning, that if they cannot afford an attorney the government will supply one, and if any of these rights are violated their confession cannot be used against them at trial.

This listing of Warren Court decisions does not suggest that this Court ignored public opinion entirely. In *Jackson v Alabama* 348 US 888 (1954), for example, Linnie Jackson, a black woman, was sentenced to five years in prison for marrying a white man, in violation of a state statute. The petition for a writ of certiorari came to the Court shortly after *Brown* and the justices probably believed that if they granted cert and ruled in favor of Mrs. Jackson it would make it more difficult to enforce the *Brown* decision. The Court denied cert and Mrs. Jackson served five years in prison. In *Naim v Naim* 350 US 891 (1955), the Warren Court also refused to hear a case in which the criminal defendant had violated a state miscegenation statute. After making this decision, one justice was supposed to have remarked, "One bombshell at a time is enough" (Murphy, 1964, p. 193). Finally, in *Loving v Virginia* 388 US 1 (1967), the Warren Court unanimously invalidated a state statute that prohibited interracial marriage. Yet, all three state statutes clearly violated the Equal Protection Clause of the Fourteenth Amendment.

Also regarding racial discrimination, the Warren Court did not in *Brown v Board of Education* 349 US 294 (1955) require school desegregation at once, even though the justices believed that desegregation was the constitutional standard. Rather, the Court used the ambiguous formula of "with all deliberate speed." In addition, the Warren Court did not rule that capital punishment was unconstitutional, even though substantial evidence was available at that time that capital punishment was being imposed by the trial courts in an arbitrary and capricious manner. It was the Burger Court in *Furman v Georgia* 408 US 238 (1972) that held that the existing state laws that allowed capital punishment were unconstitutional.[10] It is reasonable to argue regarding these Warren Court decisions that there is a limit to how far the justices are willing to go in the face of potentially strong public opposition.

The previous analysis focuses on whether the justices will avoid handing down decisions *in individual cases* because they are concerned about negative public reaction to these decisions. A good deal of the literature regarding the relationship between Supreme Court decision making and public opinion concerns whether the Court is likely to be influenced by the public mood.

McGuire and Stimson (2004, p. 1019), for example, argued that

A Court that cares about its perceived legitimacy must rationally anticipate whether its preferred outcomes will be respected and faithfully followed by relevant publics. Consequently, a Court that strays too far from the broad

---

[10] Subsequently, the Court upheld some newly enacted state capital punishment statutes but not others.

boundaries imposed by public mood risks having its decision rejected. Naturally, in individual cases, the justices
can and do buck the trends of public sentiment. In the
aggregate, however, popular opinion should still shape
the broad contours of judicial policy making.

In contrast to this *strategic model*, one can posit an *attitudinal change model* that assumes that the justices are not
influenced by the public mood but, rather, by the same forces
in society that have influenced the general public. Attitudinal
change by the justices may be a product of new appointees to
the Court, the same justices altering their attitudes, or both.
To illustrate, it is well known that the Burger Court handed
down a number of decisions that upheld the constitutional
rights of women. The strategic model would suggest that the
justices did not change their attitudes, but voted the way they
did because they believed that they ought to follow the public mood. The attitudinal change model, in contrast, would
suggest that both the justices and the general public were
influenced by the women's movement.

Giles, Blackstone, and Vining (2008) argued that if the
strategic explanation were motivating the relationship between the justices' voting and the public mood, such voting
would be present only in salient cases, in other words, only in
cases the public cares about. For no "strategic benefit accrues
to a justice who constrains his/her preferences and follows

public opinion in cases about which the public is oblivious or cares little" (p. 296). These three scholars compared Supreme Court voting in the 1976 through 1999 era with the public mood in that period, examined salient and nonsalient cases separately and, after some complex testing, concluded that

> Our results provide no support for the strategic behavior explanation.... Our results suggest that the most likely explanation for the direct linkage between public mood and justices' liberalism observed in past studies is through the mechanism of attitudinal change (p. 303).

We believe that this conclusion makes theoretical sense, for the justices are not in the business of following the public mood.

Part VI

Concluding Chapters

CHAPTER FOURTEEN

Strategies in Pursuit of Institutional Goals

Our previous discussion has focused mainly on the justices' pursuit of ideological or legal goals. Because the justices disagree regarding what ideology or interpretation of the law they favor, when an individual justice pursues her ideological or legal goals she does so at another justice's expense.

The justices, however, have shared goals as well. They want the Court to decide cases efficiently. They seek harmonious relations with each other, and they want the Court to be autonomous, influential, and respected. These shared goals are secondary goals. It is doubtful, for example, that any justice's primary goal is to have harmonious social relations on the Court or even to maximize the Court's influence. These shared goals almost certainly are not the ultimate aims of the justices. Nevertheless, the attainment of these secondary goals will often facilitate or enhance the primary goals, which are likely to be attitudinal or legal.

Strategies are often helpful in attaining these shared goals. These may be called "coordinating strategies" or, if they involve formal rules, "institutional strategies." Supreme Court scholars have not paid a great deal of attention to these strategies, but it is important to do so to understand decision making on the Court. In this chapter we argue that the following rules may make sense in light of such goals:

1.   The Rule of 4 for cert decisions
2.   Independence of the cert vote and the merits vote
3.   Rules regarding access to the Court
4.   Outcome voting
5.   The narrowest grounds rule
6.   Respect for precedent (stare decisis)
7.   Privacy and secrecy
8.   Logistics rules

The Rule of 4 for Cert Decisions

The justices have to decide how many votes are needed to grant certiorari. Because a majority vote is needed to decide the final outcome, one might suppose that the justices would adopt the same rule regarding the granting of certiorari. Instead, they require only four votes. Why did they adopt this rule? One possible reason is to give the losing litigant in the court below a greater opportunity to have his case heard. If the Court later decides that it was too lenient in granting cert, it could then vote to DIG the case (i.e., dismiss it as improvidently granted), and it could do so by a majority vote. The low rate of DIG decisions suggests that leniency is not a problem. A second possible reason for the Rule of 4 may be to emphasize the independence of the cert and the merits vote, which we will discuss later in this chapter.

It is also possible that the Rule of 4 has no effect. It may be that if granting cert required a majority vote then justices would adjust their cert voting accordingly and overall grant rates would remain about the same. If this is true, then the rule continues not because of any benefits it brings to losing litigants but, perhaps, because of the Court's concern for the independence of the cert and merits vote.

Independence of the Cert Vote and the Merits Vote

The justices keep the cert and merits votes independent. They usually do not hear oral arguments and subsequently vote on the merits on a case until months after they have voted to hear the case. These days they base their cert decisions largely on the assessment by a law clerk from the cert pool; they do so without a complete presentation of the substantive arguments in the case, without any oral presentation, and with the Rule of 4. All of these features emphasize the independence of the two decisions.

A related reason for keeping these votes independent is that by emphasizing the removal of case selection from policy considerations it may help the justices maintain control over their docket. Unlike many state supreme courts, the justices of the Supreme Court choose which cases they will hear. This control has increased over the years, culminating in 1988 in a statute enacted by Congress granting them virtually complete discretion. By implying that cases are chosen based on expertise according to legal criteria, the independence of the cert vote supports leaving the selection of their cases in the hands of the justices.

A Rules Regarding Access to the Court

After cert is granted, and if the Court does not DIG the case, the Court can still decide not to hear the substantive issue in the case (e.g., decide whether the petitioner has been discriminated against in violation of the Equal

Protection clause of the 14th Amendment). More specifically, the Court might decide that there is no access for various reasons:

1. The plaintiff in the case lacks standing, in other words, a direct personal stake in the case;
2. The case is moot, in other words, it no longer presents a live controversy;
3. The case is unripe, in other words, it is not yet ready for decision;
4. The case involves a feigned controversy or constitutes a friendly lawsuit;
5. The litigants are seeking an advisory opinion, in other words, an opinion that does not decide which litigant wins in a case, but only gives advice regarding what is the law;
6. The main issue in the case constitutes a political question, in other words, a question that ought to be decided by the president or Congress or by both political branches;
7. The case has been previously litigated by the Court;
8. The Court lacks jurisdiction over the parties or over the subject matter; or
9. The case is not justiciable, in other words, it is not appropriate for judicial determination.

In *De Funis v Odegaard* 416 US 312 (1974), for example, a white applicant was denied admission to the University of Washington Law School and claimed that if the law school had not given preference to nonwhite students he would have been admitted. De Funis argued that the failure to admit him was in violation of the Equal Protection clause of the 14th Amendment. The state trial judge agreed with De Funis and ordered that he be admitted to the law school. The case was appealed to the Washington State Supreme Court and, then, to the U.S. Supreme Court. The U.S. Supreme Court granted cert but later decided that the case was moot. At the time of his appeal, De Funis was in his final quarter of classes, and the law school had stipulated that he would be allowed to graduate regardless of how the Court decided the case. It is possible that the Court decided the case the way it did because it really believed that the case was moot, in other words, that a decision in favor of De Funis would not benefit him and that a decision against him would not hurt him. Alternatively, the Court might have used the mootness issue because it did not want to decide the preferential treatment issue at the time. Note that, despite the facts we have presented above, it is not obvious that the case was moot. De Funis might have failed one or more of the courses he was taking in his final quarter and, if this occurred, it is uncertain whether he would be allowed to graduate at the regular time or at some future date.

In any event, the access rules give the Court an additional means for not hearing cases. If these rules did not exist, the Court might have to be more careful in granting cert or might have to DIG more of the cases.

Outcome Voting

The Supreme Court uses an outcome voting rule. Cases before the Court are often multidimensional, that is, they involve two or more questions for which a justice's answers may be independent of each other. Outcome voting means that in multidimensional cases the justices do not arrive at a final decision by voting on each issue separately (known as issue voting) but, instead, vote solely on the final outcome of the case. Stearns (2000) argues that outcome voting prevents some of the voting dilemmas, in particular, cycling, that issue voting could bring.

Cycling is one of the well-known intractable voting problems that arise when voters must choose between three or more options (Arrow, 1963). It can occur with a group of as few as three members. Suppose A prefers X to Y and Y to Z (and, therefore, prefers X to Z). Suppose also that B prefers Y to Z and Z to X (and, therefore, Y to X). And suppose C prefers Z to X and X to Y (and, therefore, Z to Y). Then, a majority prefers X to Y (*A* and *C*), a majority prefers Y to Z (*A* and *B*), and a majority prefers Z to X (*B* and *C*). Thus, no matter which option is chosen, a majority of the group always prefers a different option. Condorcet, an 18th-century French mathematician, was the first scholar to identify this problem.

Cycling can arise in Supreme Court decision making when a case is multidimensional. Multidimensionality can occur whether justices are deciding cases principally on ideological grounds, legal grounds, or some combination of the two. Note that although our example above uses three options, in fact when there are two binary ("yes" or "no") issues there are four possible options: Yes and Yes, Yes and No, No and Yes, and No and No. With three issues, there are eight possible options, and, in general, with n issues there are 2^n options.

Stearns (2000) points out that issue voting, in which the justices vote on each issue separately, might result in a cycling problem. A majority, for example, might vote to reject the decision of the lower court based on one issue whereas a different majority votes to affirm it based on a different issue. Alternatively, if the case were decided sequentially, with the consequences of one issue vote determining what the next issue vote will be, then the order in which the issues were considered could affect the final outcome. Another hazard of issue voting is that the outcome can depend on how the case is divided into issues, which frequently is ambiguous.

Outcome voting avoids these problems by leaving the resolution of the issues that make up a case to the individual justices and presenting them only with a vote to affirm or to reverse the decision of the lower court, regardless of how many distinct issues are extant in a given case. Each accompanying opinion, concurrence, or dissent, of course, can discuss the individual issues as the writer wishes. One drawback to outcome voting is that in certain cases no majority opinion will be handed down. This result may create a problem for lower courts, governmental agencies, and other groups that seek to follow the Supreme Court's decision. The narrowest ground rule, which we discuss next, partially alleviates this problem by identifying the part of the plurality opinion that the lower courts must heed.

The Narrowest Grounds Rule

In some cases the decision of the Court is fractured, such that there is no majority opinion. When there is too much disagreement among the justices, they may be unable to prevent such an outcome, but it potentially affords lower courts too much discretion in how to interpret the rule of law in the case. To prevent lower courts from so taking advantage of the Supreme Court's lack of agreement, the Supreme Court has stated that lower courts should apply the narrowest grounds rule: "The holding of the Court may be viewed as that position taken by those members who concurred in the judgments on the narrowest grounds" [*Marks v United States* 430 US 193 (1977)]. Especially if, concerning a particular case, the justices' positions lie along a single ideological continuum, the justices on either end of the range would prefer the narrowest grounds decision to a decision based on the opinions at the other end of the range (Stearns 2000, p. 309).

Respect for Precedent (stare decisis)

One of the main rules of Supreme Court decision making is the obligation to conform to the precedents of the Court. The justices are not strictly bound by precedent. Rather, they have a prima facie duty to follow precedent, but the duty can be overridden if they offer a cogent reason for doing so (e.g., if they can show that the law in the former case is no longer workable or never was). This rule is known by the Latin term stare decisis or "stand by things decided."

Is there a rational basis for this rule? Brenner and Spaeth (1995, pp. 2–6) specify five values that following this rule fosters:

> Among such values are efficiency, continuity of the law, justice or fairness, legitimacy and the enhancement of the Court's decision. . . .

> First, regarding efficiency, one may argue that a de novo [or new] solution to all problems requires too much time and effort. It is much easier to simply conform to the past. As Cardozo stated, "[T]he labor of judges would be increased almost to the breaking point if every past decision could be reopened in every case, and one could not lay one's own course of bricks on the secure foundation of the courses laid by others who have gone before him." . . .

> Second, adherence to precedent also assures continuity in the law. Such continuity is often desirable because many people rely on the law in conducting their affairs. . . .

> Third, one may argue that stare decisis is fairer or more just because it treats like cases alike. . . .

> Fourth, some scholars maintain that stare decisis fosters legitimacy. Walter Murphy, for example, asserts that "When the Court reverses itself or makes new law out of whole cloth – reveals its policy-making role for all to

see – the holy rite of judges consulting a higher law loses some of its mysterious power."

Finally, some scholars contend that the justice sought to adhere to stare decisis because to do otherwise would undermine the precedential weight of their own decisions.

Concerning this fifth value, one might view stare decisis as a kind of generalized exchange (Ekeh, 1974; Takahashi, 2000) across time. The Court currently will follow previous decisions in return for the Court in the future following current decisions. It seems clear that justices would willingly give up some ability to change past decisions in return for some respect for their own decisions. Obviously no explicit, negotiated exchange between the Court in the present and the Court in the past or future is possible. Thus, the best way for the Court in the present to implement the exchange, to ensure that the Court in the future shows at least some respect for its decisions, is to unilaterally show some respect for the Court's decisions in the past, but to at the same time call attention to it and declare it a rule that the Court – which will include the Court in the future – should follow. This generalized exchange will benefit past, present, and future Courts.

Bueno de Mesquita and Stephenson (2006) contend that it may be rational for even ideologically oriented justices to respect precedent. Respecting precedent, they argue, may improve the accuracy of what the Court is saying to lower courts and so increase the likelihood the lower courts will do what the Supreme Court wants. This means, of course, that there will be a limit to how much a justice is willing to stray from his ideal position to respect precedent. "In our model, judges do not care about precedent *per se*.... An appellate judge will only vote to adhere to precedent if in doing so the legal rule can be moved sufficiently closer to the judge's ideal point that the gain in terms of accuracy is worth the cost in terms of substance" (p. 224).

Finally, Figure 14.1 illustrates a specific rationale for stare decisis discussed by Stearns (2000), again supposing that continuity in the law is desirable. Six justices (shown in bold) believe that two cases are indistinguishable and accordingly vote identically on the pair. Three justices (shown in italics) believe that the two cases are different in law and vote differently on them. The consequence is that the Court reaches opposite decisions on two cases that most justices believe to be indistinguishable. It is possible to envision, in fact, a whole series of cases in which the Court would flip-flop back and forth. Respect for precedent will prevent that. In the example, because they believe the cases are indistinguishable, if Justices 4, 5, and 6 respect precedent they will vote "pro" on the second case. The outcomes of the two cases will then be the same.

	PRO	CON
Case 1	**Justice 1**	**Justice 4**
	Justice 2	**Justice 5**
	Justice 3	**Justice 6**
	Justice 7	
	Justice 8	
	Justice 9	
Case 2	**Justice 1**	**Justice 4**
(no stare decisis)	**Justice 2**	**Justice 5**
	Justice 3	**Justice 6**
		Justice 7
		Justice 8
		Justice 9
Case 2	**Justice 1**	*Justice 7*
(with stare decisis)	**Justice 2**	*Justice 8*
	Justice 3	*Justice 9*
	Justice 4	
	Justice 5	
	Justice 6	

Figure 14.1. Flip-flopping on indistinguishable cases if precedent is not respected. Bold indicates justices who think cases are indistinguishable. Italics indicates justices who think cases are different.

Privacy and Secrecy

It is well known that the Supreme Court prizes privacy and secrecy. Oral argument, of course, is public, and those in attendance can glean information about different justices' concerns and voting inclinations from the questions the justices ask, but in conference, only the justices themselves are permitted to be present, no recording devices are allowed, and no record of any part of the proceedings is issued. There are strong norms against either the justices or the clerks revealing details of the discussions of the Court. This secrecy contrasts with official doings of legislatures, which typically are open and often are recorded. The justification for the Court's secrecy is that the legislature is doing "the people's business," which implies accountability to the people, which in turn implies transparency. The Court, in contrast, is doing "the law's business" and, therefore, is not and should not be accountable to the people.

Indeed, although the Court's secretiveness itself attracts criticism, it undoubtedly lessens criticism of other Court actions, lessens the ability of outsiders to work the Court strategically, and garners the Court more mystery and respect. In short, the Court's secretiveness is a productive strategy. It is a strategy vis-à-vis outsiders, which increases the Court's prestige and, thus, power. Although criticism of the Court's secretiveness is typically stated in terms of principles, it can be seen, in fact, as part of a power struggle, as a tactic used by outsiders to try to reduce the Court's power. The Court, not surprisingly, resists.

In part, privacy and secrecy are a strategy for the justices as a collective to deal with themselves as individuals. In the short run, it might be tempting for an individual justice to tell the outside world what is going on. It might enable her to broaden the fight against a colleague by bringing in the general public; it might be an effective way to manipulate the Court or Congress on a particular issue; or it simply might bring her attention and publicity. In the long run, however, less secretiveness probably would weaken the Court and thereby all the justices. In short, for individual justices there may be temptations to give out information that ultimately would diminish the Court's power and would harm the group as a whole. This rule solves that social dilemma.

Related to these reasons, Justice Frankfurter has argued that invading "the privacy of the conference room ... would have a chilling effect on the frank exchange of views among the justices" (Dickson, 2001, p. 15). In addition, Justice Powell has pointed out that "secrecy allowed the Justices to be more flexible in deciding cases than if their conference votes were immediately made public" (Dickson, 2001, p. 15). In fact, the immediate public disclosure of the justices' conference votes might discourage them from shifting their votes during the course of the decision-making process. In other words, it would interfere with reasoned decision making by the justices.

Logistics Rules

Meetings. Much of the justices' work they do on their own or with their law clerks, but they do things with each other as well, of course, and so they have regular meeting times. This strategy is one of coordination. There is more to it, however, for they have additional rules concerning their meetings. Their first meeting of the new term takes place in the week before the first Monday in October. The Court typically hears cases in an alternating pattern of a two-week sitting, during which they hear oral arguments, and a two-week recess when they work on cases. Oral arguments are heard only between 10 AM and 3 PM on Monday through Wednesday. This is sufficient because, unless the solicitor general has filed an amicus brief, each side of a given case is almost always allotted exactly 30 minutes for its presentation. On Fridays, the justices meet in conference to vote on cases and cert petitions. By May they are finished with hearing cases, so that in May and June they meet only to issue orders and opinions. Typically they finish their work by the end of June.

Almost all of these rules are arbitrary. They could hear cases Tuesday through Thursday, for example, or do one-week sitting, one-week recess, but all of those rules eliminate the effort and possible conflict that would be involved in arranging meetings. They have a schedule and rules for the schedule, which in fact they did not ever have to create but simply inherited it from earlier Courts, and it coordinates them nicely. The rule of most recent origin is the time limits on oral arguments, and clearly is a strategy for dealing with cases efficiently, that is, minimizing the time they have to devote to this activity.

We might ask, also, why all of these meetings are necessary. Aside from the public hearings of the cases, they certainly could accomplish much of their decision-making work without meeting, and most people do not like meetings. The likely answer is that the justices choose to hold their meetings as a way of binding themselves (see Heath, 2006) and each other. Without the meetings, some justices probably would be tardy, perhaps very tardy, submitting their votes and arguments, just as some justices are with their written opinions.

Hierarchy. The formal hierarchy in the Supreme Court was adopted in the first session of the first U.S. Congress: There would be one chief justice and associate justices. Congress has assigned to the chief justice administrative duties that the other justices do not have to perform. The Court itself has created an additional determinant of hierarchy – seniority – and the other duties and privileges of hierarchical position. This creation and use of hierarchy is another coordination strategy for a group. The chief justice, for example, is the moderator for the Court's conference. He initiates the Discuss List of cases to be considered for certiorari. He typically represents the Court when it seeks favors from Congress. Although these duties give the chief justice more power, they also accomplish tasks that otherwise might not get done well.

Seating. Where the Supreme Court justices sit may not seem like a strategy but it is, albeit not a hugely consequential one. The two formal settings are the public sittings where the justices hear the cases and the conferences where they decide them. At both they have set seats. At the public sittings they are in a row, with the chief justice in the middle, flanked by the associate justices according to seniority, so that the most junior justices are on the outside. At the conferences, they are seated around a rectangular table, with the chief justice at the head of the table. The most junior member of the Court sits at the end of the table closest to the door.

How is seating a strategy? Set, hierarchically organized seats at the public sittings reinforce the dignity and thus the prestige of the Court. In the private conferences, it emphasizes the hierarchy and removes a chance for small tensions between members.

The Discuss List. The Discuss List is an example of a strategy in the form of an institutional rule developed to ensure productive use of the Court's time together. The Court receives a huge number of petitions for certiorari. In 2004, for example, it received 2041 paid petitions and 6543 *in forma pauperis* or unpaid petitions (Epstein, Segal, Spaeth, and Walker, 2007, Table 2–6), yet the total number granted was 69 paid petitions and 11 unpaid ones. Clearly, a great deal of pruning of the petitions must be done by the justices, and the procedure they have adopted is the Discuss List. The chief justice circulates a list of the petitions to which he believes the Court might consider granting cert; other justices add any other cases they want. Any case that does not make it onto this Discuss List is automatically denied cert.

The Discuss List enables the Court to focus on a minority of the petitions, ones they are all prepared to discuss. The strategic nature of this rule is especially clear from its history. When few petitions were received, there was no rule – there was no need for it. As the number of petitions increased, however, a dead list was created, of petitions the justices could agree to ignore. Thus, the justices would not waste time and preparation on cases none of them would want to hear. As the volume of petitions continued to increase, it became simpler to list the cases that at least one of the justices did *not* want to ignore, hence, the Discuss List.

Opinion Assignment. The rule concerning the appointment of the majority opinion writer is another example of a coordination strategy. If the chief justice is a member of the conference coalition, he either self-assigns the majority opinion or assigns it to another justice in the conference coalition. If the chief justice is not a member of the conference coalition, the most senior justice on the coalition assigns the majority opinion.

Clearly, the rule privileges the chief justice, and is inegalitarian as well in that it favors the most senior justice if the chief justice is not a member of the conference coalition. The strategic value of having such rules, however, is that they eliminate the effort of negotiation and the potential for conflict in the selection of the majority opinion writer. Other rules would be possible, but perhaps would be less preferred by most justices. A rotation scheme, for example, could be used either for the writing of the majority opinion or for its assignment. The former, however, is highly undesirable because it ignores all the variables that might be relevant in preferring Justice A to write the majority opinion in a given case rather than Justice B. The latter is undesirable if the chief justice or the senior associate justices have better judgment than the other justices regarding who ought to write the majority opinion. In the long run, the seniority rule is not unfair in that justices will tend to become more senior as time goes on, if they are still on the Court. The rule that privileges the chief justice is simply a perquisite of being chief justice.

CHAPTER FIFTEEN

Summary

In Chapters 5 through 14 of this book we have explored whether the justices on the Court behave strategically. What have we discovered? We first examine the evidence that the justices are not behaving strategically:

1. In cases granted cert by the Court, reverse-minded justices do not vote in accord with the outcome-prediction strategy. Affirm-minded justices in the aggregate do so, but only about half of the individual affirm-minded justices pursue this strategy. In cases denied cert by the Court, the justices do not vote in conformity with this strategy (Chapter 5).

2. Even though Chief Justice Burger, at times, voted insincerely and with the majority at the conference

vote on the merits, there is no evidence that the associate justices on the Court voted this way (Chapter 6).

3. Although we identified some possible strategic reasons for justices changing their votes between the conference vote and the final vote, the justices almost always shift their votes for nonstrategic reasons, for example, because they have changed their mind regarding which outcome they favor or because they were in the minority at the conference vote and wish to conform to the majority (Chapter 7).

4. Successful bargaining over the content of the majority opinion between the majority opinion writer and the other members of the conference coalition took place in less than 6 percent of situations on the Burger Court (Chapter 8).

5. Majority opinion coalitions usually are not minimum winning (MW) (Chapter 9).

6. The majority opinion is usually not written at the ideal point of the median justice on the Court, even when that justice is a member of the conference coalition (Chapter 10).

7. Justices, even justices of similar ideological orientation, are unlikely to join each other's opinions at the same rate. This is particularly true regarding concurring and dissenting opinions, for some justices

are more likely to be writers, whereas other justices are more likely to be joiners (Chapter 11).

8. Since the early 1940s the justices have been less likely to cast unanimous final votes (Chapter 11).

9. The Court does not typically vote against its preferred outcome in statutory cases to avoid a possible congressional override (Chapter 12).

10. The Court does not usually vote against its preferred outcome in an individual case to avoid a possible negative reaction by the general public. The Court, in addition, usually does not follow the public mood. Rather, it may be influenced by the same events in the society that influence the general public (Chapter 13).

In contrast, we also discovered some evidence that the justices are behaving strategically:

1. A certain amount of strategic behavior takes places at the cert vote (Chapter 5).

2. The majority opinion writer is less likely to alter his opinion to satisfy the other justices in the conference coalition after he obtains an MW vote for his opinion (Chapter 9).

3. The majority opinion writer is more likely to write his opinion at the ideal point of the median justice in the conference coalition than at the ideal point of the

justice ideologically closest to the majority opinion writer (Chapter 10).

4. Throughout most of Supreme Court history, the justices tended to cast unanimous final votes (Chapter 11).

5. The justices follow various strategies in pursuit of institutional goals (Chapter 14).

In addition to these five findings, an opinion assigner behaves strategically when he assigns the opinion to himself or to an ideological ally, if we assume that the majority opinion writer will want to and be able to write the opinion at his ideal point or close to it.

Also, we know that in MW conference coalitions the marginal justice (i.e., the justice ideologically closest to the dissenters) is favored in opinion assignment (Brenner and Spaeth, 1988). Although it is uncertain why this justice is favored, it is reasonable to argue that she is favored for strategic reasons, for example, because the assigner believes that such assignment will encourage her to remain in the coalition.[11]

---

[11] Whether, in fact, the opinion assigner is able to achieve this goal is problematic. Brenner, Hagle, and Spaeth (1989, p. 417) found no evidence that the marginal justice in a MW conference coalition is less likely to defect when assigned to write the majority opinion. Lax and Rader (2008, p. 19) discovered that "being assigned to write the majority opinion has a small negative effect on defection." They did not, however, ascertain whether this finding also pertains to MW conference coalitions.

Summary

Based on our mixed results, we believe that it is a mistake to characterize the justices on the Court as strategic actors, who take advantage of their strategic positions to achieve their legal or policy goals. Strategic behavior occurs on the Court, but it takes place much less often than the strategic scholars claim.

Note

In Appendix 2 we have presented a number of questions concerning Supreme Court behavior that the student might explore with strategic and other theoretical tools.

Decision Making on the
United States Supreme Court

To understand these chapters it is necessary to know some-thing about the procedures involved in decision making on the Court. We present a short summary of these procedures.

1. The Supreme Court receives requests for review by a number of methods. The most common method is a petition for a writ of certiorari. Certiorari (cert) peti-tions are of two kinds: paid petitions, in which the petitioner pays the required fees, submits the appro-priate number of copies, and follows the other guide-lines for submission; and petitions *in forma pauperis* (i.e., in the form of a pauper), mostly submitted by fed-eral and state prisoners, in which the fees and most of the other requirements are waived.

2. The cert petitions are typically filed by a litigant who has lost in a U.S. Court of Appeals or in a state supreme court.

3. The cert petitions are read by a law clerk from the cert pool and by a law clerk from Justice Steven's office (who does not read all of them). The law clerks read the petition and the lower court record, prepare a memo that summarizes the case, and recommends whether cert ought to be granted or denied.

4. With the help of his law clerks, the chief justice prepares a list of cases to be placed on the Discuss List. Any other justice can add a case to the list. Any case not placed on the Discuss List is automatically denied cert.

5. The justices meet in secret conference to decide whether to grant or to deny the petitions of the cases on the Discuss List. The justices vote in order of seniority, with the chief justice voting first, the senior associate justice (in terms of tenure on the Court), voting second, and so on. If eight or nine justices are voting, it takes four votes to grant cert. But if only six or seven are voting, it takes three votes.

6. The justices have complete discretion regarding whether cert petitions ought to be granted or denied. The Supreme Court also receives requests for review

by petitions for a writ of appeal. Although these petitions are called "mandatory," the justices, in reality, also have complete discretion whether to hear these petitions or not.

7. Even after granting cert, the Court can DIG a case (i.e., dismiss it as improvidently granted). The Court does not DIG cases very often. It takes five votes to DIG a case.

8. The Court summarily disposes of a large percentage of the cases to which it grants cert. In other words, the Court decides to grant cert and also decides the case on the merits, without written briefs, oral argument, or the writing of a majority opinion.

9. In cases granted cert and given full consideration (or full treatment) by the Court, the attorney for the petitioner has 45 days from the time the Court grants review to file a written brief on the merits. The attorney for the respondent has 30 days from the time he receives the petitioner's brief to file his brief. Interested third parties or interest groups (known as amicus curiae) may get permission from the litigants or from the Court to file briefs as well.

10. The attorneys for both sides also participate in oral argument. Oral argument, except regarding a few salient cases (e.g., *Bush v Gore*) lasts one hour, equally

divided between the attorneys for both sides. When the solicitor general has filed an amicus brief, someone from his office also presents his position at oral argument.

11. After oral argument the justices meet in secret conference to decide whether to reverse or to affirm the decision of the lower court. This vote is called *the conference vote on the merits*. The justices present their views and vote in order of seniority, with the chief justice voting first. It takes a majority vote to reverse or affirm. If the vote is 4–4 (or 3–3), the decision of the lower court is affirmed without opinion.

12. The winning coalition at the conference vote is called *the conference coalition*. The chief justice, if he is a member of the conference coalition, assigns the majority opinion. He can self-assign the majority opinion or assign it to any other justice in the conference coalition. If the chief justice is not a member of the conference coalition, the senior associate justice (in terms of tenure on the Court) in that coalition makes the assignment.

13. A justice can change her vote (e.g., shift from reverse to affirm or the converse) at any time prior to the announcement of the Court's decision in open court. At times, the Court shifts its votes as well. A shift by the

Court may require the reassignment of the majority opinion.

14. The justice assigned to write the majority opinion usually obtains at least four additional votes for the opinion and, as a result, he is able to hand down an authoritative opinion of the Court (also called the majority opinion). If he fails to do so, he hands down a plurality opinion (known officially as a Judgment of the Court).

15. The other justices may write or join a regular concurring opinion, a special concurring opinion, or a dissenting opinion. Although a justice who writes or joins a *regular* concurring opinion is also joining the majority or the plurality opinion, this is not true regarding a justice who writes or joins a *special* concurring opinion.

16. The Court announces its decision in open court and submits the various opinions to the media and other interested groups. The coalition that wins at the final vote on the merits is called *the decision coalition*, and the coalition that supports the majority or the plurality opinion is called *the opinion coalition*. An opinion coalition can be the same size as the decision coalition, it can be smaller, but it cannot be larger.

Additional Questions to Explore

There are a host of additional questions that can be explored with strategic and other theoretical tools. Consider the following:

1. Why have recent Courts granted cert to many fewer cases than in the past? During the 1970 through the 1978 terms, for example, the Court granted cert to more than 200 paid petitions per term (Epstein, Segal, Spaeth, and Walker, 2007, Table 2-6). In contrast, in the 1992 to 2007 era it never granted cert to 100 paid petitions in any term. Is it surprising that the justices do not hear as many cases as possible?

2. Why does the Court grant cert to cases "that do not possess any political significance" (Cross, 1998, p. 559)?

3. Why does the Court grant cert to many cases they affirm (Cross, 1998, p. 560)? Is this the best use of the Court's resources?

4. If the justices cast four votes to grant cert and five to deny cert, why do the five rarely vote to DIG (dismiss it as improvidently granted) the case (Segal and Spaeth, 2002, p. 435)?

5. "Given the advantage of speaking first and voting last, why in the world did the Chief Justice even begin voting first" (Segal and Spaeth, 2002, p. 435)? Note that the change took place when Warren was chief justice.

6. Brenner and Spaeth (1988) inspected minimum winning (MW; 5–4, 4–3) conference coalitions on the Warren Court and discovered that the marginal justice (i.e., the justice ideologically closest to the dissenters) was assigned to write the majority opinion more than twice as many times than can be expected based on random assignment. Why is this justice favored in this situation?

7. Why does the marginal justice in a MW conference coalition almost always join the majority opinion? Why does he not, instead, write a special concurring

opinion, particularly when that opinion is likely to set forth the law in the case (Cross, 1998, p. 548)?

8. Why does the Court not issue advisory opinions (Cross, 1998, p. 556)?

9. Why do the justices limit themselves to deciding the issues raised by the litigants (Cross, 1998, p. 556)?

10. Why do the justices not time their retirement so that they will retire when they are likely to be replaced with justices who share their ideological orientation?

References

Arrington, Theodore S. and Saul Brenner. 2004. "Strategic Voting for Damage Control on the Supreme Court." *Political Research Quarterly* 57:565–574.

Arrington, Theodore S. and Saul Brenner. 2008. "Testing Murphy's Strategic Model: Assigning the Majority Opinion to the Marginal Justice in the Conference Coalition on the U.S. Supreme Court." *American Politics Research* 36:416–432.

Arrow, Kenneth J. 1963. *Social Choice and Individual Values*. New York: Wiley.

Baum, Lawrence. 1997. *The Puzzle of Judicial Behavior*. Ann Arbor: University of Michigan Press.

Baum, Lawrence. 2006. *Judges and Their Audiences: A Perspective on Judicial Behavior*. Princeton, NJ: Princeton University Press.

Baum, Lawrence. 2007. *The Supreme Court*. 9th ed. Washington, DC: CQ Press.

References

Baum, Lawrence and Lori Hausegger. 2004. "The Supreme Court and Congress: Reconsidering the Relationship." In Mark C. Miller and Jeb Barnes (Eds.), *Making Policy, Making Law: An Interbranch Perspective*, pp. 107–122. Washington, DC: Georgetown University Press.

Benesh, Sara C. 2003. "Harold J. Spaeth: The Supreme Court Computer." In Nancy Maveety (Ed.), *The Pioneers of Judicial Behavior*, pp. 116–147. Ann Arbor: University of Michigan Press.

Black, Duncan. 1958. *The Theory of Committees and Elections*. Cambridge: Cambridge University Press.

Blaustein, Albert P. and Roy M. Mersky. 1978. *The First One Hundred Justices*. Hamden, CT: Archon Books.

Bonneau, Chris W. and Thomas H. Hammond. 2005. "Do We Really Know It Because We See It? Reconceptualizing 'Strategic Behavior' on the United States Supreme Court." Paper presented at the Annual Meeting of the American Political Science Association, Washington, DC, Sept. 1–4.

Bonneau, Chris W., Thomas H. Hammond, Forrest Maltzman, and Paul J. Wahlbeck. 2007. "Agenda Control, the Median Justice, and the Majority Opinion on the U.S. Supreme Court." *American Journal of Political Science* 51:890–905.

Boucher, Robert L. Jr. and Jeffrey A. Segal. 1995. "Supreme Court Justices as Strategic Decision Makers: Aggressive Grants and Defensive Denials on the Vinson Court." *Journal of Politics* 57:824–837.

Braman, Eileen and Thomas E. Nelson. 2007. "Mechanism of Motivated Reasoning? Analytical Perceptions in

Discrimination Disputes." *American Journal of Political Science* 51:940–956.

Brenner, Saul. 1975. "The Shapley-Shubik Power Index and Supreme Court Behavior." *Jurimetrics Journal* 15:194–205.

Brenner, Saul. 1979a. "The New Certiorari Game." *Journal of Politics* 412:649–655.

Brenner, Saul. 1979b. "Minimum Winning Coalitions on the United States Supreme Court: A Comparison of the Original Vote on the Merits with the Opinion Vote." *American Politics Quarterly* 7:384–392.

Brenner, Saul. 1989. "Fluidity on the United States Supreme Court: A Reexamination." In Sheldon Goldman and Austin Sarat (Eds.), *American Court Systems*, 2nd ed., pp. 479–483. New York: Longman Inc.

Brenner, Saul. 2003. "David Rohde: Rational Choice Theorist." In Nancy Maveety (Ed.), *The Pioneers of Judicial Behavior*, pp. 270–288. Ann Arbor: University of Michigan Press.

Brenner, Saul and Theodore S. Arrington. 1980. "Some Effect of Ideology and Threat Upon the Size of Opinion Coalitions on the United States Supreme Court." *Journal of Political Science* 8:49–58.

Brenner, Saul and Robert Dorff. 1992. "The Attitudinal Model and Fluidity Voting on the United States Supreme Court: A Theoretical Perspective." *Journal of Theoretical Politics* 4:195–205.

Brenner, Saul, Timothy Hagle, and Harold J. Spaeth. 1989. "The Defection of the Marginal Justice on the Warren Court." *Western Political Quarterly* 42:409–425.

References

Brenner, Saul and John F. Krol. 1989. "Strategies in Certiorari Voting on the United States Supreme Court." *Journal of Politics* 51:824–840.

Brenner, Saul and Harold J. Spaeth. 1988. "Majority Opinion Assignments and the Maintenance of the Original Coalition on the Warren Court." *American Journal of Political Science* 32:72–81.

Brenner, Saul and Harold J. Spaeth. 1995. *Stare Indecisis: The Alteration of Precedent on the Supreme Court, 1946–1992*. New York: Cambridge University Press.

Brenner, Saul and Joseph M. Whitmeyer. ND. "At Whose Ideal Point Will the Majority Opinion Be Written on the United States Supreme Court?" Unpublished paper, on file, University of North Carolina, Charlotte, Department of Sociology.

Brenner, Saul, Joseph M. Whitmeyer, and Harold J. Spaeth. 2006. "The Outcome-Prediction Strategy in Cases Denied Review by the U.S. Supreme Court." *Public Choice* 130:225–237.

Bueno de Mesquita, Ethan and Matthew Stephenson. 2006. "Informative Precedent and Intrajudicial Communication." In James R. Rogers, Roy B. Flemming, and Jon R. Bond (Eds.), *Institutional Games and the U.S. Supreme Court*, pp. 205–229. Charlottesville: University of Virginia Press.

Caldiera, Gregory A. and John R. Wright. 1988. "Organized Interests and Agenda Setting in the U.S. Supreme Court." *American Political Science Review* 82:1109–1128.

Cameron, Charles M., Jeffrey A. Segal, and Donald R. Songer. 2000. "Strategic Auditing in a Political Hierarchy: An Informational Model of the Supreme Court's Certiorari Decisions." *American Political Science Review* 94:101–116.

References

Campbell, Jeremy. 2001. *The Liar's Tale*. New York: W.W. Norton.

Collins, Paul M. Jr. 2008. "The Consistency of Judicial Choice." *Journal of Politics* 70:861–873.

Cross, Frank B. 1998. "The Justices of Strategy." *Duke Law Journal* 48:511–569.

Dickson, Del. 2001. *The Supreme Court in Conference (1940–1985): The Private Discussion Behind Nearly 300 Supreme Court Decisions*. New York: Oxford University Press.

Dorff, Robin H. and Saul Brenner. 1992. "Conformity Voting on the United States Supreme Court." *Journal of Politics* 54:762–775.

Downs, Anthony. 1957. *An Economic Theory of Democracy*. New York: Harper.

Ekeh, Peter P. 1974. *Social Exchange Theory: The Two Traditions*. Cambridge, MA: Harvard University Press.

Epstein, Lee and Jack Knight. 1998. *The Choices Justices Make*. Washington, DC: CQ Press.

Epstein, Lee, Jeffrey A. Segal, Harold J. Spaeth, and Thomas G. Walker. 2007. *The Supreme Court Compendium: Data, Decisions, and Developments*. 4th ed. Washington, DC: CQ Press.

George, Tracy E. and Lee Epstein. 1992. "On the Nature of Supreme Court Decision Making." *American Political Science Review* 86:323–337.

Gerhart, Michael J. 2008. *The Power of Precedent*. New York: Oxford University Press.

Gibson, James L., Gregory A. Caldiera, and Lester Kenyatta Spencer. 2003. "Measuring Attitudes Toward the United

References

States Supreme Court." *American Journal of Political Science* 47:354–367.

Giles, Micheal W., Bethany Blackstone, and Richard L. Vining Jr. 2008. "The Supreme Court in American Democracy: Unraveling the Linkages between Public Opinion and Judicial Decision Making." *Journal of Politics* 70:293–306.

Gillman, Howard. 1999. "The Court as an Idea, Not a Building (or a Game): Interpretive Institutionalism and the Analysis of Supreme Court Decision-Making." In Cornell W. Clayton and Howard Gillman (Eds.), *Supreme Court Decision-Making: New Institutional Approaches*, pp. 65–87. Chicago: University of Chicago Press.

Green, Donald P. and Ian Shapiro. 1994. *Pathologies of Rational Choice Theory: A Critique of Applications in Political Science*. New Haven, CT: Yale University Press.

Hagle, Timothy M. and Harold J. Spaeth. 1991. "Voting Fluidity and the Attitudinal Model of Supreme Court Decision Making." *Western Political Quarterly* 44:119–128.

Hammond, Thomas H., Chris W. Bonneau, and Reginald S. Sheehan. 1999. "Toward a Rational Choice Spatial Model of Supreme Court Decision-Making: Making Sense of Certiorari, the Original Vote on the Merits, Opinion Assignment, Coalition Formation and Maintenance, and the Final Vote on the Choice of Legal Doctrine." Paper presented at the Annual Meeting of the American Political Science Association, Atlanta, Sept. 2–5.

Hansford, Thomas G. and David F. Damore. 2000. "Congressional Preferences, Perceptions of Threat and Supreme Court Decision Making." *American Politics Quarterly* 28:490–510.

References

Hansford, Thomas G. and James F. Spriggs II. 2006. *The Politics of Precedent on the U.S. Supreme Court*. Princeton, NJ: Princeton University Press.

Hausegger, Lori and Lawrence Baum. 1999. "Inviting Congressional Action: A Study of Supreme Court Motivations in Statutory Interpretations." *American Journal of Political Science* 43:162–185.

Heath, Joseph. 2006. "The Benefits of Cooperation." *Philosophy and Public Affairs* 34:313–351.

Hettinger, Virginia A. and Christopher Zorn. 2005. "Explaining the Incidence and Timing of Congressional Responses to the U.S. Supreme Court." *Legislative Studies Quarterly* 30:5–28.

Howard, J. Woodford, Jr. 1968. "On the Fluidity of Judicial Choice." *American Political Science Review* 62:43–56.

Howard, Robert M. and Jeffrey A. Segal. 2002. "An Original Look at Originalism." *Law and Society Review* 36:113–138.

Johnson, Timothy R., James F. Spriggs II, and Paul J. Wahlbeck. 2005. "Passing and Strategic Voting on the United States Supreme Court." *Law and Society Review* 39:359–377.

Johnson, Timothy R., Paul J. Wahlbeck, and James F. Spriggs II. 2006. "The Influence of Oral Arguments on the U.S. Supreme Court." *American Political Science Review* 100:99–113.

Kritzer, Herbert M. and Mark J. Richards. 2003. "Jurisprudential Regimes and Supreme Court Decision Making: The Lemon Regime and Establishment Clause Cases." *Law and Society Review* 37:827–840.

Kritzer, Herbert M. and Mark J. Richards. 2005. "The Influence of Law in the Supreme Court's Search-and-Seizure Jurisprudence." *American Politics Research* 33:33–55.

References

Lax, Jeffrey R. and Charles M. Cameron. 2005. "Beyond the Median Voter: Bargaining and Law in the Supreme Court." Paper presented at the Annual Meeting of the Midwest Political Science Association, Chicago, April 7–10.

Lax, Jeffrey R. and Kelly T. Rader. 2008. "Bargaining Power in the Supreme Court." Paper presented at the Annual Meeting of the Midwest Political Science Association, Chicago, April 3–6.

MacDonald, Paul K. 2003. "Useful Fiction or Miracle Worker: The Competing Epistemological Foundations of Rational Choice Theory." *American Political Science Review* 97:551–566.

Maltzman, Forrest, James F. Spriggs II, and Paul J. Wahlbeck. 1999. "Strategy and Judicial Choice: New Institutionalist Approaches to Supreme Court Decision-Making." In Cornell W. Clayton and Howard Gellman (Eds.), *Supreme Court Decision-Making: New Institutionalist Approaches*, pp. 45–63. Chicago: University of Chicago Press.

Maltzman, Forrest, James F. Spriggs II, and Paul J. Wahlbeck. 2000. *Crafting Law on the Supreme Court: The Collegial Game*. New York: Cambridge University Press.

Maltzman, Forrest and Paul J. Wahlbeck. 1996. "Strategic Policy Considerations and Voting Fluidity on the Burger Court." *American Political Science Review* 90:581–592.

Maltzman, Forrest and Paul J. Wahlbeck. 2004. "A Conditional Model of Opinion Assignment on the Supreme Court." *Political Research Quarterly* 57:551–563.

Marks, Brian. 1989. "A Model of Judicial Influence on Congressional Policy-Making: Grove City v Bell." Ph.D. dissertation, Washington University, St. Louis, MO.

References

McGuire, Kevin T. and James A. Stimson. 2004. "The Least Dangerous Branch Revised: New Evidence on Supreme Court Responsiveness to Public Preferences." *Journal of Politics* 66:1018–1035.

Molm, Linda D. 1997. *Coercive Power in Social Exchange*. Cambridge: Cambridge University Press.

Murphy, Walter F. 1964. *Elements of Judicial Strategy*. Chicago: University of Chicago Press.

Murphy, Walter F., C. Herman Pritchett, Lee Epstein, and Jack Knight. 2006. *Courts, Judges, and Politics: An Introduction to the Judicial Process*. 6th ed. New York: McGraw-Hill.

O'Brien, David M. 2005. *Storm Center: The Supreme Court in American Politics*. 7th ed. New York: Norton.

Perry, H. W. Jr. 1991. *Deciding to Decide: Agenda Setting in the United States Supreme Court*. Cambridge, MA: Harvard University Press.

Posner, Richard A. 1995. *Overcoming Law*. Cambridge, MA: Harvard University Press.

Posner, Richard A. 2008. *How Judges Think*. Cambridge, MA: Harvard University Press.

Pritchett, C. Herman. 1948. *The Roosevelt Court: A Study of Judicial Politics and Values, 1937–1947*. New York: Macmillan.

Provine, Doris Marie. 1980. *Case Selection in the United States Supreme Court*. Chicago: University of Chicago Press.

Richards, Mark J. and Herbert M. Kritzer. 2002. "Jurisprudential Regimes in Supreme Court Decision Making." *American Political Science Review* 96:305–320.

Rohde, David W. 1972. "Policy Goals and Opinion Coalitions in the Supreme Court." *Midwest Journal of Political Science* 16:208–224.

References

Rohde, David W. and Harold J. Spaeth. 1976. *Supreme Court Decision Making*. San Francisco: W.H. Freeman.

Rosen, Jeffrey. 2006. *The Supreme Court: The Personalities and Rivalries That Defined America*. New York: Henry Holt.

Schotter, Andrew. 2006. "Strong and Wrong: The Use of Rational Choice Theory in Experimental Economics." *Journal of Theoretical Politics* 18:489–511.

Schubert, Glendon. 1958. "The Study of Judicial Decision Making as an Aspect of Political Science." *American Political Science Review* 52:1007–1025.

Segal, Jeffrey A. 1997. "Separation-of-Powers Games in the Positive Theory of Law and Courts." *American Political Science Review* 91:28–44.

Segal, Jeffrey A. and Harold J. Spaeth. 2002. *The Supreme Court and the Attitudinal Model Revisited*. New York: Cambridge University Press.

Segal, Jeffrey A., Harold J. Spaeth, and Sara C. Benesh. 2005. *The Supreme Court in the American Legal System*. New York: Cambridge University Press.

Songer, Donald R., Charles M. Cameron, and Jeffrey A. Segal. 1995. "An Empirical Test of the Rational-Actor Theory of Litigation." *Journal of Politics* 37:1119–1129.

Spiller, Pablo. 2000. "Review of *The Choices Justices Make*, by Lee Epstein and Jack Knight." *American Political Science Review* 94:943–944.

Spriggs, James F. II, Forrest Maltzman, and Paul J. Wahlbeck. 1996. "We Have a Deal: Strategic Tactics on the Supreme Court." Paper presented at the Annual Meeting of the Midwestern Political Science Association, Chicago, April 18–20.

References

Spriggs, James F. II, Forrest Maltzman, and Paul J. Wahlbeck. 1999. "Bargaining on the U.S. Supreme Court: Justices' Responses to Majority Opinion Drafts." *Journal of Politics* 61:485–506.

Stearns, Maxwell L. 2000. *Constitutional Process: A Social Choice Analysis of Supreme Court Decision Making*. Ann Arbor: University of Michigan Press.

Takahashi, Nobuyuki. 2000. "The Emergence of Generalized Exchange." *American Journal of Sociology* 105:1105–1134.

Time. 1972. "The Supreme Court: Deciding Whether to Decide." December 11, 72 and 77.

Toobin, Jeffrey. 2005. "Annals of Law: Breyer's Big Idea." *New Yorker*, October 31:36–40, 42–43.

Ulmer, S. Sidney. 1970. "The Use of Power in the Supreme Court: The Opinion Assignments of Earl Warren, 1953–1970." *Journal of Public Law* 19:49–67.

Wahlbeck, Paul J., James F. Spriggs II, and Forrest Maltzman. 1996. "Marshalling the Court: Bargaining and Accommodation on the U.S. Supreme Court." Paper presented at the Annual Meeting of the Western Political Science Association, San Francisco, CA, March 14–16.

Westerland, Chad. 2003. "Who Owns the Majority Opinion?" Paper presented at the Annual Meeting of the American Political Science Association, Philadelphia, PA, August 28–31.

Westerland, Chad. 2004. "Cooperative Norms on the U.S. Supreme Court." Paper presented at the Annual Meeting of the American Political Science Association, Chicago, IL, Sept. 2–5.

References

Yamagishi, Toshio and Karen S. Cook. 1993. "Generalized Exchange and Social Dilemmas." *Social Psychology Quarterly* 56:235–248.

Zorn, Christopher J. W. 2002. "U.S. Government Litigation Strategies in the Federal Appellate Courts." *Political Research Quarterly* 55:145–166.

Table of Cases

Index

Index

Index

Index

merits votes, 48
  independence of, 141–142
Mersky, Roy, 64
minimum winning (MW) vote model,
  81–86
  in racial discrimination cases, 85
  in threat cases, 82
Miranda v Arizona, 131, 190
miscegenation laws, 132. *See also Jackson
  v Alabama; Loving v Virginia; Naim v
  Naim*
Molm, Linda, 104
motivated reasoning, of justices, 6
multidimensionality in cases, 146
Murphy, Walter, 17, 35, 41, 54, 71, 83,
  94, 122
Murray v Curlett, 130
MW votes. *See* minimum winning vote
  model

NAACP. *See* National Association for the
  Advancement of Colored People
Naim v Naim, 132, 190
narrowest ground rule, 147–148
National Association for the
  Advancement of Colored People
  (NAACP), 35
"natural" courts,
  conference votes in, 57
Nelson, Thomas, 6, 8
New Deal, 21

O'Brien, David, 55
O'Connor, Sandra Day, 56
opinion coalition, 171
outcome-prediction strategy, 39–50, 161
  strategic auditing in, 40
  writ of certiorari in, 39–40
outcome voting, 145–147

Parsons, Ed, xi
Pennsylvania v Muniz, 56, 190
Perry, H. W. Jr., 49
petitioning costs, 34
Posner, Richard, 13, 27
Powell, Lewis, 98, 154
prayer in public schools, 130–131. *See
  also Abington v Schempp; Engel v
  Vitale; Murray v Curlett*

preemptive accommodation, 77
principal-agent problem, 32–33, 36
Pritchett, C. Herman, 11, 17, 35, 41, 54,
  94, 122
Provine, Doris Marie, 49
public opinion, on Supreme Court
  decisions, 127–135, 163
  attitudinal model and, 134
  on Bill of Rights cases, 129
  on capital punishment, 133
  on criminal defendants' rights, 131
  on desegregation, 130
  on free speech, 131
  on miscegenation laws, 132
  on prayer in public schools,
    130–131
  strategic model and, 133–134

racial discrimination cases
  Brown v Board of Education, 65
  MW vote model for, 85
Rader, Kelly, 164
rational choice models, 21–26
  advantages of, 25
  benefits v. costs in, 24
  consistency requirements in, 22
  criticism of, 22–24
  equality within, 22
  utility maximization in, 21–22
reciprocity, in Supreme Court,
  103–112
  theory of exchange and, 104–107
Reed, Stanley F., 43
Rehnquist, William, 13, 43, 98
reverse discrimination, 144. *See also De
  Funis v Odegaard*
Richards, Mark, 7
Roberts, John G., 112
Rohde, David, 26, 81, 82–84, 86, 87. *See
  also* minimum winning vote
  model
Rosen, Jeffrey, 112
Rule of 4, for Supreme Court justices,
  140–141
  DIG decisions and, 141

Scalia, Antonin, 13
Schotter, Andrew, 24, 25
Schubert, Glendon, ix

Index

Index